CALLED TO SOMETHING
GREATER

SPIRIT REIGN
PUBLISHING
A Division of Spirit Reign Communications

DARRELL A. PALMES III

CALLED TO SOMETHING
GREATER

Author: Darrell A. Palmes III
Cover design: David Anderson
Page design & layout: Ornan Anthony of OA.Blueprints, LLC
Editor: Spring Hawk Publications

© 2013 Spirit Reign Communications. All rights reserved. No part of this publication may be reproduced, stored in a retrieval system, or transmitted, in any form or by any means, electronic, mechanical, photocopying, recording, or otherwise, without the prior written permission of the copyright holder.

Printed in the United States of America

ISBN PB: 978-1-940002-22-4
ISBN ePDF: 978-1-940002-24-8
ISBN ePUB: 978-1-940002-23-1

SPIRIT REIGN
PUBLISHING
A Division of Spirit Reign Communications

CONTENTS

Dedication..4

Acknowledgements..5

Preface...6

Introduction..8

Chapter 1: Jeremiah's Story..13

Chapter 2: My Story..19

Chapter 3: What's Your Story (Discover Your Greatness).35

Chapter 4: Faith to Pursue Your Greatness......................53

Chapter 5: Mental Toughness..63

Chapter 6: Transitioning to Your Greatness......................73

Chapter 7: Criticism from Others....................................83

Chapter 8: Support System..97

Chapter 9: Look the Part..105

Chapter 10: Procrastination..117

Chapter 11: Finish Strong...129

Chapter 12: THE Something Greater..............................137

DEDICATION

To Robyn, Brittany, and Darrell IV (Daddy's CHAMP), you are WHY I GRIND!
Love you!

To my birth mother, Gwendolyn T. Palmes "…and the dead in Christ shall rise first."
1 Thessalonians 4:16-18.

As long as my family and I are there to meet you and Jesus in the air, it was all worth it.

ACKNOWLEDGEMENTS

To my God and King, most of all, my Savior: You put up with a lot from me, yet you still called me? I simply say thank You! I'll love and serve You forever—not because of what You've done, are doing, and continue to do—but because of who You are.

To my parents: Darrell Palmes and Beryl White, and also my siblings: Catina and Winston. We're not a perfect family, but we're just that—family.

To all of my nieces and nephews: Uncle Darrell expects greatness from you!

Eric Thomas – I never dreamed this book was inside of me. Your encouragement pushed me to something greater. Thanks bro!

To the "Prayer Line" brothers: You know who you are!

To my focus group: Thanks for your support. Your input helped make this book better.

To my publishers, Spirit Reign Communications & Publishing: Thanks for your support. Ready for the next one?

PREFACE

The following are terms you'll become familiar with as you read this book.

Calling - as defined by the Merriam-Webster Dictionary is: *A strong inner impulse toward a particular course of action, especially when accompanied by conviction of divine influence.*

According to this definition, most people acknowledge their calling as one that is divinely inspired. Once you have acknowledged your special calling, it will be necessary for you to begin that *journey toward a particular course of action;* one that will lead to the revelation of your calling.

Dream - definition 4a according to the Merriam-Webster Dictionary is: *A strongly desired goal or purpose; a dream of becoming president.*

Some of you have different dreams and/or aspirations in life. Hopefully, this book will drive you to not only dream, but dream big, and then live that dream.

In this book, you'll notice that these terms are often

used interchangeably. In some cases, however, there can be differences between the two. For example, God's calling on your life can be dramatically different from the dreams you have for yourself. God may be calling you to become a doctor but you may have dreams of becoming an actor. While it's true that if you *"delight thyself also in the Lord; and He shall give thee the desires of thine heart"* (Psalm 37:4), the goal for the reader of this book is to seek to have your dreams align with God's will. Your dreams may not necessarily be bad ones. According to scripture, there is a way to be sure that your dreams line up with God's will. 1 John 4:1 states, *"Beloved, believe not every spirit, but try the spirits whether they are of God..."* In other words, when your relationship with God is strong, the dreams you have should match His will for your life. If you have not yet developed a strong relationship with Him, as you continue to read, you'll have the opportunity to.

INTRODUCTION

Before I formed thee in the belly I knew thee; and before thou camest forth out of the womb I sanctified thee, and I ordained thee a prophet unto the nations.
Jeremiah 1:5 (KJV)

I have no doubt that you are called to do something great. Whether you envisioned that greatness spiritually, academically, or professionally, you desire more for your life. I'd even go so far as to say that you are willing to do anything to fulfill that yearning.

This book was born during a season in my life when I wanted nothing more than to fully operate in the calling God placed on my life. Having been replaced as pastor of the church I planted, and losing my job a few days later, I wondered what God's plans were—considering all the things in my life that weren't going the way I imagined they would.

In this book, I will briefly explore the life of Jeremiah the Prophet. We will examine the call that God placed upon him, and find similarities that apply to us. From this, we will see how that call is similar to the call that God has given to us. I will also step outside of my comfort zone and tell you a little bit about my life. It is my prayer that you acknowledge and accept the call that God has placed upon your life. Better days will result for you once you do.

This book is designed for those who are confident that they have been called to something greater but, for whatever reason, are not yet walking in that call. It is my desire that as you read this book and implement the concepts, you will be filled with the Spirit and have the boldness necessary to pursue your dreams. In case you're wondering what qualifies me to present these concepts to you, please continue reading and your question will undoubtedly be answered. I will not share my entire life-story but I will share enough to give you insight into the preparation process God had me go through, which demanded I write this book.

In the first 3 chapters I will deal with three stories; Jeremiah's, mine, and yours. In chapters 4-11, we will get into the concepts necessary to propel you into the greatness that God has for you. Chapter 12 will bring everything together and, hopefully, challenge you to want to pursue your call to something greater with tenacity the world has never seen before.

I want to encourage you that just like I didn't give up, you shouldn't give up either. Don't settle for being just a dreamer, get to a point where you begin to live your dreams! After all, you are Called to Something Greater!

"Dreams come a size too big so that we can grow into them." -Josie Bissett

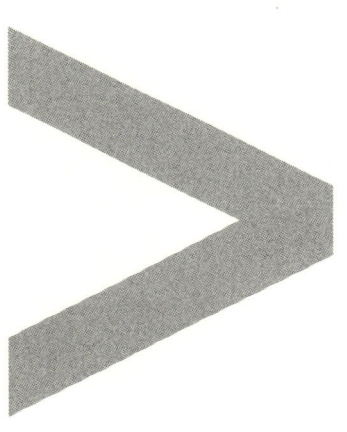

DARRELL A. PALMES III · **11**

CHAPTER 1
JEREMIAH'S STORY

And they shall fight against thee; but they shall not prevail against thee; for I am with thee, saith the Lord, to deliver thee.
Jeremiah 1:19 (KJV)

Jeremiah, the son of a priest, was from the tribe of Levi and was preparing to become a priest himself. This preparation process started at an early age. But God was about to interrupt Jeremiah's plans. The Lord spoke directly to Jeremiah with these words: *"Before I formed thee in the belly I knew thee; and before thou camest forth out of the womb I sanctified thee, and I ordained thee a prophet unto the nations."* [Jeremiah 1:5].

Can you imagine hearing directly from God? Now imagine not only hearing from God, but hearing Him tell you the specific plans He has for your life. Wow! Based on what the scriptures tell us, Jeremiah responded to the Lord in a way I'm sure most of us would respond. Jeremiah said, *"...Ah, Lord God! behold, I cannot speak; for I am a child..."* [Jeremiah 1:6]. Now, some adults might think that you wouldn't say to the Lord that you are a child, but let's examine that for a moment.

Think about having a conversation with God about His plans for your life. What if God's plan leads you somewhere you've never been before? What if God wants you to fulfill your purpose by taking on a task or something in which you have no experience? Since you would be inexperienced moving forward in your call, it's conceivable that you could be considered "childlike" as it relates to your call since you would essentially have to learn something brand new.

God responded to Jeremiah, declaring, *"...Say not, I am a child: for thou shalt go to all that I shall send thee, and whatsoever I command thee thou shalt speak."* [Jeremiah 1:7]. These words should offer some encouragement to us today. It's obvious God does not want us to focus on our inability to do what He calls us to do. Too often we rely on our own strength and ability to accomplish things. But what I have found to be true on several occasions is that God will often place someone in a situation where their own ability is of no use. The reason for this is so that we can learn to place our complete trust in God at all times. That way, He alone receives credit for the success.

God further encourages Jeremiah saying, *"Be not afraid of their faces: for I am with thee to deliver thee, saith the LORD." [Jeremiah 1:8].* Have you ever told someone that you were about to embark on something and the look on their face discouraged you from wanting to continue? Don't worry about the opinions or perception of others as it relates to your calling. Yes, they will look at you strangely. Yes, they will talk about you. Yes, they will laugh at you. But God promises that He will be with us and He will deliver us. I don't know about you, but knowing that God will be with me every step of the way and provide the strength necessary to keep moving ahead gives me the courage to go and pursue His plans for my life.

Here's further proof that God will give us strength: *"Then the LORD put forth his hand, and touched my mouth. And the LORD said unto me, Behold, I have put my words in thy mouth." [Jeremiah 1:9].* Talk about a confidence booster! God is saying to us that when He calls us, we don't even have to come up with our own words or methods. He promises to give us *everything* we need to get the job done; we'll discuss that momentarily, but I challenge you here to go with God. If you do, you'll have everything you need to arrive at your call to something greater sooner rather than later.

CHAPTER RECAP

During the final 40 years of the existence of Judah as a kingdom, Jeremiah preached messages of revival and repentance during the reign of five kings. Though his message was not always well-received, Jeremiah was faithful to his calling as a prophet. In spite of all the negativity and rejection he received, he still followed the Lord wholeheartedly. You and I should do the same. Regardless of where God is leading us in life, it is always better to remain faithful to Him.

"Success certainly isn't achievement of popularity. Success in God's kingdom is loving God, loving one another, and being faithful to what He's called us to do."
- Gabriel Wilson

JEREMIAH'S STORY

DARRELL A. PALMES III · **17**

GREATER>

CHAPTER 2
MY STORY

Fear thou not; for I am with thee: be not dismayed; for I am thy God: I will strengthen thee; yea, I will help thee; yea, I will uphold thee with the right hand of my righteousness.
Isaiah 41:10 (KJV)

My childhood was very troubled—I was kicked out of several schools because of my behavior. I believe some of my behavioral issues stemmed from certain aspects of my home life. My mother died when I was a little over a year old. My father soon remarried the woman I call Mom to this day. My early years at home were okay, and I believe they formed the foundation for the spiritual life I have now.

My entire family (which included my father, mother, older sister and brother), had family worship every morning, and every Friday evening we celebrated the Sabbath together. Sabbath observers typically honor God's rest from creation as found in Genesis 2:1-3. The Fourth Commandment found in Exodus 20:8-11, tells us to remember the Sabbath day and to keep it holy.

My parent's relationship did not last and I became the product of a broken home. My sister and brother went to live with my mother, and I lived with my dad.

I had not yet reached double-digits (as far as age was concerned) and had already lost my birth mother, stepmother, my sister and brother. Growing up in a single parent home with just my father was cool, but I'm sure you can imagine how lonely I felt most of the time. I believe the loneliness is what caused me to get into trouble. By age ten, I had already experimented with smoking, sex, and other things no ten-year-old should be involved with.

I have always looked older than my true age, and I used that to my advantage. It enabled me to get things that I felt I needed in order to "survive." My father and I never had heart-to-heart conversations, and now I realize how important it is for fathers and sons to discuss life issues. It's vital that parents begin pouring wisdom into their sons and daughters at an early age. It's crucial to not only be a disciplinarian but also a friend and companion to your children. Frequently, I hear parents say, *"I'm not your friend; I'm your parent."* This way of thinking can be detrimental in many ways. Yes, you are parent *first* and *foremost*. But by you not wanting to be your child's friend, he or she will find friends elsewhere. I don't want to give the impression that my father was a *bad* father. Yes, I believe he made bad decisions at times, but who hasn't made bad decisions before? Some have made more than others, but we've all made them nonetheless. That puts us all on the same playing field.

My father remarried; by that time, I was completely into doing my own thing. I couldn't have been more than 12 years old, but I was acting like I was 16 because I felt I needed to handle things on my own. My father was out making a living to provide for the family. Even though my new stepmother was present (as well as a couple of cousins who had come to live with us), I still felt like I was on my own. I didn't have many friends during that period in my life. I've never been one to play the role of a victim, I figured smoking weed and drinking alcohol would help me cope with my feelings.

At that point, I had been arrested and locked up several times. There's much more I could share about my childhood but, suffice it to say, it was more than rough. Admittedly, it was rough both voluntarily and involuntarily. I say voluntarily because I willingly did things in response to the things I was experiencing. I'd like to encourage whoever is reading this and experiencing feelings similar to those I felt. No one can make you do anything. Everything is a choice. Even though things around you may seem to be crumbling, it's how you respond to these things that will determine where you end up in life.

I was again kicked out of school, and by 16, I was virtually homeless. The fact that I looked older worked to my advantage; I got a job at a major corporation. Since I looked older, I had to sound older also in order to sell the lie. I told my employers I was 19 when in reality I was only 16. I was soon fired from that job because my immaturity caused me to get into it with another employee. You see, some things I could mask very well but at the end of the day, no matter how mature a 16-year-old may seem, he's still 16. Such was the case with me.

From about age 16 to 19, I was totally homeless. I would try to stay with certain friends and relatives but that was short lived. Many nights I slept outside. Sometimes I'd sleep at a train station, or wherever my feet stopped after walking the streets midnight and early morning. To tell you how bad it was at times, I would even go to some of my relative's homes and knock on the door only to have them reject my knocks, which resulted in me sleeping outside on their porches. Then, I *really* started smoking and drinking because getting high and drunk seemed to be the only thing in my life I could depend on.

For the life of me, I couldn't figure out why I was going through such hard times at such an early age. I would ask myself questions like, *"How did I end up here?"* I vividly remember having to steal clothes from department stores, and skipping out on restaurant checks just to make sure I had clothes to wear and food to eat. I would also steal from grocery stores and other establishments just to survive. On some occasions, I even stole from relatives (hoping they wouldn't notice the missing money, clothes, shoes, etc...) because I felt that I had reached a place in my life where it was either survive or die. Throughout all of this, even though I was discouraged most days because I didn't know how I was going to recover, I still knew there had to be more in store for my life. I just didn't know what it was.

Somehow, I had managed to get back on my feet, not knowing that God was with me the whole time. I was blessed to get a couple of jobs, which allowed me to eventually get a car and my own apartment. I thought I had finally moved on to better days, but God was not finished with my process yet.

I lost one of my jobs and the other one, which was working security, wasn't giving me enough hours to pay all of my bills. I was one month behind on my rent but I kept going to work and tried to do everything I could to come up with the rent money. My car broke down while coming home from a graduation I attended in Huntsville, AL, so I was now taking the bus and train to and from work.

I had a strange feeling on the way to work one day as I was walking past the leasing office toward the bus stop. I felt as though the people in the leasing office were watching me. I proceeded to get on the bus and go to work. After working all day, I came home on the bus and started walking toward my apartment. While approaching my apartment, I remember seeing a sweater on the ground that looked a lot like mine. I also saw an ironing board that looked familiar. I thought - 'there's no way those things on the ground could be mine and proceeded to put the key in my door. After trying it several times, the key still would not open the door. I went back outside and took a closer look at the items only to discover they were, in fact, mine. *"Are you kidding me?"* I couldn't believe I was still experiencing this awful string of bad luck.

Follow me here. I lost one of my jobs, my car broke

down, and now I was evicted from my apartment. How could this be happening to me? Just when I thought my life was turning around, this happened. You can't tell me that God wasn't up to something! Going back a little bit, I was always getting high. My family would ask me why I smoked so much marijuana, but they didn't know all the things I was going through at the time. In all honesty, I used drugs and alcohol recreationally, but they were also a coping mechanism. It seemed to be the only thing I could depend on while I was going through the turmoil.

Fast-forward to 2003. I began my professional career working in the IT field. Although I held jobs prior to this in various places such as grocery stores, fast food restaurants, and other customer service related roles, IT was my "career" choice. In 2003, I decided to obtain certifications verifying that I was able to work on computers. Once I completed these certifications, I immediately got a job in the IT field as a help desk representative for a major corporation. I answered the calls of individuals who were experiencing hardware and software problems with their computers. This job was so great I ended up getting several of my classmates' jobs with this company also. This wasn't intended to be the last stop in our IT endeavors but the experience definitely didn't hurt us moving forward—especially just having graduated. It takes most people months, if not years, to find a job after finishing school so I considered this position to be a blessing that I had to share with others.

Shortly after leaving that job, I was blessed to get another job traveling to various parts of the country fixing computers. I got this job toward the latter part of 2003, shortly after finishing school. I thought it was the best job ever! I was able to travel to different places and not only receive a paycheck but also an expense check! Sometimes, my expense check was equal to or even greater than my actual paycheck. I knew I had found my place. But then life happened. I quickly found out that the work I was doing was on a contract basis. While contractors can make great money, they don't have much stability. So, once the contract ends you're looking for work again. The wait between contracts could be very long; sometimes weeks or even months. God always provided for me and I would be blessed with a job just when I needed it the most.

In 2005, I got married, and 16 months later, in 2006, I received an offer to work on a contract for the federal government. It was a long-term contract opportunity. Most of my colleagues had been employed on this contract for more than 10 years, and I was confident this would be the last stop in my career. However, God had other plans for my life.

In the middle of 2007, I distinctly remember a Voice telling me to write a sermon. I remember laughing out loud because the Voice I heard was so crystal clear. It was as if someone was in the room talking to me. This Voice was none other than the Holy Spirit. Some refer to the Holy Spirit as their conscience—I concur with this. God, through the Holy Spirit, speaks to us telling us what is right and wrong. God has given all of us freedom of choice so it's entirely up to the individual whether or not they listen to this "inner voice". That day, I chose to listen to the Holy Spirit. I suggest here that with every decision you face, seek to listen to the voice of the Holy Spirit and you'll never go wrong.

I won't get into too much detail here, but I *will* say that my lifestyle prior to and even during the preparation of this sermon was not a lifestyle deemed fit or proper for someone delivering a sermon. I remember it was summertime when I began preparing this sermon. I didn't finish it until December, which goes to show you I had no knowledge of what I was doing! Around November of that year, I was invited to preach at a church for their Youth Day in December.

I figured God was using this as an opportunity to finish that sermon so I could preach it. As I write this, I'm laughing to myself and thinking how if I had never received that speaking engagement, I would never have finished that sermon!

I invited all my friends and family to come hear the sermon because it was a grand day for me. Having lived the lifestyle I'd lived and then to be preaching a sermon... wow! I didn't want anyone to miss that day. I preached the sermon to the best of my ability, listened to the opinions of those who heard it and then casually went on about my business—working my job as usual.

Coming from a background where having the knowledge to do multiple jobs was a necessity, working in a traditional "9 to 5" was never my passion. I had plans to open businesses and explore various professional ventures that would lead to financial gain. But the money I was making in IT caused me to put some of those dreams on hold. Plus, I didn't have all the capital necessary to branch out and pursue those enterprises. But with every idea, I kept hearing that same Voice that told me to write the sermon say *"You can move forward with your plan, but I have something else for you to do."*

I had my doubts before but, by then, I definitely knew that was the voice of God. I was amazed that God would want to speak to me. I mean, I was going to church and returning my tithes and offerings as I was supposed to do, but I was also battling my sins. So, not being a perfect Christian, I couldn't see why God was speaking to me so clearly. When God spoke to me previously, it was usually Him telling me not to do this or that, but having God speak to me about my future was different. I kept inquiring of God as to what it was He would have me do and finally, in January of 2008, one month after preaching my first sermon, God in this same crystal clear voice told me He wanted me to become a pastor. "Are you for real?" I asked. I remember asking God several times on that Sunday night if He was serious about me becoming a pastor. Every time I would ask Him a question regarding this special calling He had reserved for my life, He would always respond in the affirmative, letting me know that this was the call to something greater that was for me. I not only ended up pastoring a church, God had me start the church I pastored.

You see, it doesn't matter what you are doing, where you are doing it, why, or even how you are doing it, when God calls you the only thing that matters is that you respond to His calling. The wonderful thing I love about God's call upon everyone's life to something greater is that it doesn't matter who you are or what you've done. Everyone has something special to do on this earth, and when God is with you, rest assured that as long as you adhere to the call that is inside of you, you will eventually walk in that calling.

Once I reached the point of total surrender to God's call on my life, His plans became so much clearer to me. I decided that if I was going to become a pastor I could no longer smoke and drink... *(Actually, I stopped smoking tobacco New Year's Eve 2000. A young lady I was dating at the time whom I'd met during a Homecoming weekend at Oakwood University said that if I wanted to be with her, I couldn't smoke anymore. Naturally I was willing to stop smoking because this woman was so beautiful that...well, you get the point!)* I wasn't really smoking that much weed during this period in my life because of my job. I still drank quite a bit though because at that time, I didn't see anything wrong with it. Needless to say, the call on my life demanded a total lifestyle transformation. So, I ask you, does the call on your life require a complete transformation? I'd say no matter what your calling is, it will demand total change. But we'll discuss more on that later.

I was still working in the IT field because, after all, this was my source of income. I want to encourage you, dear reader, to put your faith in God rather than your employer. Remember that God was the One who blessed you with your job in the first place. Since He blessed you with it, should He desire to move you somewhere else, be open to His leading. I realize for some, having a "regular" job is the only way you know how to survive. But I want to direct your attention to Philippians 4:19 that says, *"But my God shall supply all your need according to His riches in glory by Christ Jesus."* It is not your job that supplies your needs it is Christ. You may be very successful in your career, but your success is not built on a sure foundation unless you depend on Him fully.

CHAPTER RECAP

Once I accepted the call to ministry in 2008, I discovered that even though I was still working in the IT field, my mind was always drawn to ministry. I was continuing to work in an area that was outside of my calling. God used me in IT during that season in my life but He was still calling me to something greater. I wanted to fulfill that calling but I wasn't trusting God enough to leave my job and pursue my call full time. Listen very carefully to what I am about to say: I am in no way suggesting that you go out and quit your job to pursue the greatness that is inside of you. There are times when God will reveal to you His plans for your life, but He needs you to continue serving Him and others; being faithful where you are before He elevates you to the next level. For me, I knew that God did not want me to continue working in IT as my primary focus. While I am still qualified to work in the IT arena, I am now seeking to shift my vocational abilities and qualifications to using them in the ministry that God has called me to. However, for some of you, your occupation is your calling.

The point I want to stress is that before you begin to pursue your call to something greater, make sure you pursue the One who called you in the first place. Mark 10:27 states, "And Jesus looking upon them saith, 'With men it is impossible, but not with God: for with God all things are possible.'" Don't try to accomplish great things using your own strength. Always go in the strength of God.

"Do not spoil what you have by desiring what you have not; remember that what you now have was once among the things you only hoped for."
- Epicurus

<GREATER>

CHAPTER 3
WHAT'S YOUR STORY
(DISCOVER YOUR GREATNESS)

> *For I know the thoughts that I think toward you, saith the LORD, thoughts of peace, and not of evil, to give you an expected end.*
> *Jeremiah 29:11 (KJV)*

Jeremiah's discovery of His greatness came almost immediately after the Lord called him. While everyone may not experience the same realization as soon as Jeremiah did, it's imperative that you discover what God would have you do as soon as possible; doing so can save you a lot of time and energy.

From childhood, most people have had some idea of what they wanted to be when they grew up. It may have been a policeman, fireman, pastor, doctor, lawyer, chef, or some other profession. You probably had dreams of great success in the profession of your choosing. My father was an accountant. I remember his clients ranged from huge corporations to small families trying to keep their finances in order. What I remember most, is that my father made a decent living doing what he loved. The fact that he was so successful led me to want to become a CPA also. I wanted to experience a similar lifestyle. But more than that, I wanted to be like my father. Seeking to become like your heavenly Father is also important as I'll share momentarily.

During the early phases of my elementary education, however, I learned very quickly that I did not like math. I struggled in certain areas, but I somehow found a way to persevere. Once I entered Pre-Algebra, I knew that being an Accountant was no longer in my future. For the life of me I couldn't figure out why letters were appearing in my mathematical equations! In my mind, there was no reason for a, b, c, x, or y to equal anything. So after realizing that accounting was not in my future, I had to decide upon another profession. After all, I knew I had to do something as an adult, I just didn't know what that something was. I had a feeling I was called to do something great but I had no clue what that "great" thing was, nor did I know how to achieve it.

You see, all of us have something inside of us that we are destined to do. The Bible lets us know in Jeremiah 29:11 that God has a plan for each of our lives. He has called us to do great things for Him while we are on this earth. If you did not have anything left to do for Jesus, you would not be alive. Since you are still in the land of the living, you have a purpose and that purpose is to become the best you can be.

Since you're reading this book, you must have similar feelings. You feel that you have been called to do something great. You may even feel that the greatness inside of you is destined to change the world. But for some reason, even though you have a "feeling" that you have been called to greatness, there's a problem: you don't exactly know what it is you're supposed to do; or, you know what it is you're supposed to do but you don't know how to manifest what's inside of you for the world to see. The steps that I will outline in this book have worked for others and they are definitely working for me. It is my prayer that as you continue reading and implementing what is written in these pages, you will not only discover the greatness that awaits you but you will also be able to tap into that greatness and begin living a life that is filled with purpose—on purpose.

SEEK GOD
The first step in achieving your call to something great is acknowledging that you have a great God

inside of you. The Bible tells us in 1 John 4:4 that, "...*greater is He that is in you, than he that is in the world.*" Please do not miss this point. If the Spirit of God is dwelling inside of you then you have no choice but to be great! The simple fact that you have a feeling that something great is in you should propel you to seek that greatness, and that seeking begins with God. Before you can obtain and live in greatness, you have to be willing to submit yourself to the Greatest. Look at the text again. "*...greater is He that is in you, than he that is in the world.*" There are forces in this world that will do anything to prevent you from obtaining your call to something greater. We'll get into some of those forces later on in this book, but rest assured, there is an enemy out there just waiting to keep you from walking in victory. But the promise has been given to us that if we seek the Lord we shall not lack any good thing (Psalm 34:10, NKJV). Achieving your greatness must begin with seeking Someone greater than you are, and that Someone is Jesus Christ.

One of the best ways that I have sought God is by rising early in the morning to walk and talk with Him. I have found that there is something special about seeking God early in the morning. Lately, I have been getting up around 4:30AM each morning to seek the face of God. I wasn't always an early riser. I used to believe that getting up an hour or so before work, saying my prayers, and then getting ready for the workday ahead was enough. I mean, I would constantly talk with God throughout the day. I would pray on the way to work, while sitting in traffic, while at work to get guidance on how to handle customers and co-workers, driving home and then before I went to bed that evening. I didn't see the need to get up early for prayer when I was making it my business to commune with God through the day. But it was after I connected with some friends on a prayer line that I would soon be convinced that early risers for the purpose of walking and talking with God received special blessings from their heavenly Father that other people did not have.

I invited a friend to come and preach for me one weekend to culminate our youth emphasis month at a Church I was pastoring at the time. After a Spirit-filled day that included morning and evening worship, my friend began to prepare for another engagement he had the following day. He advised me on some of the challenges I was facing in my life. After praying over these things, he asked me what time I usually woke up in the morning. I told him I was having an incredibly hard time waking up at a decent hour. He then gave me one of those responses that a doctor would give you after you told them what the reason was for your appointment. "So I see," he said. He then invited me to join a prayer line that was comprised of men who wanted to become the godly men that Christ intended, and that it began at 6:30AM the following Monday. He told me to dial in at 7:00AM instead. I told him that time would be a stretch for me but I consented. You see, whenever you are going to do something that will make you better, it will require you to stretch yourself. In other words, if you desire different results in your life you're going to have to make the choice to do something different.

I dialed in to the prayer line number at 7:00AM as agreed. Since it was my first time on the call I didn't want to speak out of turn. So I listened intently to what was being discussed and prayed to the Lord for guidance as to whether this was something I wanted to be a part of each morning. After all, I needed my rest and I wasn't about to jeopardize my precious sleep for foolishness. The call lasted a few hours which was ironic to me considering that most prayer lines are only open for about 15 minutes to an hour at most. But this prayer line was different. It wasn't just filled with the prayers of other men; there were discussions taking place about real life issues that men, husbands, and fathers face. These issues were dissected, examined carefully under a spiritual microscope. Then biblical advice was given on how to handle these issues. I sensed that the Spirit of God was on this prayer line as breakthrough after breakthrough would occur in the lives of these men. I called my friend later on and told him how blessed I was to have been a part of something like this and proceeded to let him know that I would seek to get on the call again the next day, only this time, I would try to join at the regular start time.

A few months passed and I was still connecting to the prayer line each morning. I felt I was growing spiritually as a result but I knew there was something more I had to do. Although this prayer line provided me the spiritual boost I needed, it was not enough. There were a couple of guys connected to the prayer line, my friend included, who consistently got up even earlier than the start time for the call; anywhere from 2:00AM to 5:00AM. I thought that was insane in the beginning. They told me the purpose for them getting up earlier was to seek the face of God in their lives in an intimate, one-on-one style that resembled the life of Enoch (Genesis 5:24). I could see that God was rewarding them with blessing after blessing because of their deliberate pursuit of Him.

I decided to try this since I was at a place in my life where I wanted to go deeper in my walk with Christ. However, I had an issue with setting the alarm on my cell phone and efficiently hitting the snooze button whenever it went off. I then began to ask God to wake me up when He wanted me to get up so as not to rely on the alarm on my cell phone. This way, I was relying on God to wake me up as opposed to an alarm clock—since God is the one who gave me the ability to hear the clock in the first place. I didn't know what I was asking for because the Lord answered my prayer quickly by waking me up earlier than I could've ever imagined.

I can honestly say that getting up around 4:30AM and sometimes earlier to seek God's face has truly changed my life! The Lord has given me such insight and direction on where He wants to take me. And, because of that, I am pursuing the greatness inside of me even more so, now that I know God is with me. He was with me all along but now that I know Him more intimately, I have a better understanding of what He requires of me. Each day I am still seeking to know Him better. Knowing that I am called to something greater because He has given me the vision of greater is simply awesome. My advice to you would be to seek God early in the morning and you will literally watch your life change. If you are serious about obtaining your call to something greater, ask God to wake you up just 30 minutes earlier and then spend that time seeking His face. That time can be spent in various ways like going for a walk in your community while praying, studying the Bible, reading a good devotional book, listening to Christian music, or utilizing any other method you desire that will help you commune with God more intimately. I would also recommend going to bed at least thirty minutes to an hour earlier than you are normally accustomed to so as to ensure you receive the proper amount of rest. Remember, if you want a different result, you'll need to do something different. Seek the face of God and I guarantee He will reveal to you the great things He has planned for you.

SUBMIT TO GOD
Once you have sought the Lord, it is now necessary to submit to him. Searching for the Lord is not as easy as utilizing your favorite Internet search engine as if to research information for a school report, and once the report has been turned in, you go back to living life the same way you were before you began your search. The journey does not end with the search; you have to move from search to submission and then, ultimately, to obedience.

Too often, people seek the Lord only for what they can get out of Him as if He were some magic genie in a bottle. They go to God and present their three wishes to Him and expect those wishes to come true. Then once we receive the blessings or wishes, we kindly ask or even *expect* God to go back inside the bottle and come out again when we have need of Him. If we are being honest with ourselves, how often do we seek the *hand* of God, as opposed to the *face* of God? It is only when we seek the face of God and seek to be like Him that we will be truly on our way to seeing the greatness that is inside of us manifested. The proof of this is found in 2 Chronicles 7:14 which states: *"If my people, which are called by my name, shall humble themselves, and pray, and seek my face, and turn from their wicked ways; then will I hear from heaven, and will forgive their sin, and will heal their land."*

I have discovered that when you submit to the will of God, it allows you to clearly identify the will and call that He has placed on your life. So many people look to psychics, horoscopes, and other methods to determine their place in this world. Jeremiah 29:11 clearly states that God not only knows the plans He has for us, but that His plans call for us to prosper in the future. Now if you feel that those other methods work for you, then carry on with those. But I have come to the conclusion that since there is a God in Heaven who knows more about me than I know about myself, I'll choose His plans for my life any day.

I mentioned earlier that true submission to God would lead to obedience to God. We should seek to be obedient to God not because of what He will give to us in return, but for no other reason than because we love Him. The Bible says in Ephesians 2:8-9, *"For by grace are ye saved through faith; and that not of yourselves: it is the gift of God: Not of works, lest any man should boast."* In other words, our works, (in this case, our obedience to God), doesn't necessarily save us in and of itself. If you're a parent, it's just like telling your children that if they were to clean their room you would give them an allowance or some other reward. So, because there's an incentive for them, they wouldn't be cleaning their room because it is the right thing to do they would be cleaning it for the reward associated with it. Such is also the case in our relationship with Christ. We shouldn't desire to obey God because it could lead to a promotion on our jobs, larger banks accounts, newer vehicles, a bigger home, or any other perk. Our obedience to Him should come from a heart that desires to please our heavenly Father. The more seasoned Christians say it this way:

"If God never does anything else for me, He has already done enough!" Just as you want your children to be obedient to you regardless of gain or recompense, good or bad, the same should apply to us as it pertains to our relationship with Christ. You should want to be obedient to the Lord because He loves you and you have the ultimate trust that He will never lead you down the wrong path, just like you would desire for your children as it relates to their obedience towards you. Don't seek to obey God because of what He might do for you. Obey Him because you love Him. Submit and surrender your all to God today and trust that you are in the best hands possible.

DOMINION

Once you have submitted your will to the will of God, it is important for you to understand the principle of dominion. During the creation of the world, God gave us dominion over all that He created. The Bible says in Genesis 1:1-2, *"In the beginning God created the heaven and the earth. And the earth was without form, and void; and darkness was upon the face of the deep. And the Spirit of God moved upon the face of the waters."* The text illustrates how God spoke the sun, moon, and stars into existence, as well as the beautiful and lush garden vegetation that would make our eyes water at the sight of its splendor. Then, after all of the animals were created and danced gracefully around their newly formed habitats, the Lord made a special declaration in verse number 26 of Genesis chapter 1: "*And God said, Let us make man in our image, after our likeness: and let them have dominion over the fish of the sea, and over the fowl of the air, and over the cattle, and over all the earth, and over every creeping thing that creepeth upon the earth.*" Notice how clear this text is. After God created everything that we could ever have needed, He created us. Everything else was spoken into existence with the exception of man. God chose to create us with His own hands. Genesis 2:7 asserts, "*And the Lord God formed man of the dust of the ground, and breathed into his nostrils the breath of life; and man became a living soul.*" Man was the final masterpiece during the six literal days of creation. It was on the sixth day of creation that God gave us dominion over everything that had been spoken into existence during the previous five days.

Allow me to ask a question: Since God has given us dominion over the entire earth, why do some of us settle for being dominated? Some of us are dominated by our sinful proclivities; dominated by our bills and debt; dominated by our negative thinking; or even dominated by others. If we are to truly obtain the victories that God has for us we need to understand that an unwavering person who is fully committed to doing the will of Christ should never allow themselves to be dominated. Dominion means to reign or rule over something. As long as you have the Spirit of God inside of you (see 1 John 4:4) nothing can stand in your way, unless you allow it to.

Some of you are even being dominated by your jobs. Don't get me wrong, having a job is a blessing. However, since God has given us a mandate to have dominion, I believe that we are actually supposed to create jobs, as opposed to simply working a job. Again, having a job is a tremendous blessing. However, I choose to believe a bigger blessing comes when we work full-time on building the dreams that God has given us as opposed to working full-time building someone else's dream.

To have dominion means you need to have the confidence to know that anything is possible simply because of your position. Consider this for a moment: Do you think the President of the United States or any other leader is unclear about their leadership role or has difficulty understanding that they have dominion in the country in which they serve? We'll save the discussion on how they choose to exercise that dominion for another time, but I need you to understand the point. The very seal of the President of the United States declares his name, title, and territory of authority. The same is true with our heavenly Father. Exodus chapter 20:11 states: *"For in six days the Lord made heaven and earth, the sea, and all that in them is..."* God's seal, as found in Exodus 20:11 declares His name (which is *Lord*), His title, which is *Creator* (the text says that He *made*), and His territory, *(heaven and earth, the sea and all that in them is)*. You may be thinking how this relates to you. Psalm 8:6 further illustrates my point by declaring: *"Thou madest him to have dominion over the works of thy hands; thou hast put all things under his feet:"* So if all things are to be under our feet, it's time to start acting like it! Depression, doubt, fear, laziness, or any other excuse that you have used in the past for not going after God's call to greatness on your life needs to be placed underneath your feet. If you practice living a life of dominion and making no apologies for it along the way, and recognize that the Creator of the universe gave you that power, you'll soon be on your way to discovering the greatness inside of you.

CHAPTER RECAP

Some of you who are reading this book know that you have been called by God to do something great, but you don't know exactly what it is that you are supposed to be doing. Then there are those of you who are approaching this book with an idea of what that greatness is that God has called you to; however, you simply need to obtain the knowledge and guidance on how to go about securing your call to something greater. Whatever category you fall into, please understand that God has a special plan for your life. He created you with a purpose. You are such a unique individual that no one else on this earth can do what you have been called to do. Others may have a similar calling but no one can do it quite like you can because God only made one you! The way that you preach, sing, cook, teach, practice medicine, argue cases in the courtroom, negotiate deals in the boardroom, etc., your specific call to greatness can only be achieved by you. Once you understand the importance of seeking the face of God wholeheartedly, submitting to His will for your life above your own desires, and then understanding that you were created to have dominion over the earth, God will reveal to you the plans that He has for your life. The blessing contained within this principle is having the knowledge that as long as you have God on your side, nothing shall be impossible for you. Are you ready to discover your greatness? If so, then know that whatever you discover on this journey is yours!

"We may seek God by our intellect, but we can only find Him with our heart."
- Cotvos

GREATER>

CHAPTER 4
FAITH TO PURSUE YOUR GREATNESS

*Now faith is the substance of things hoped for,
the evidence of things not seen.
Hebrews 11:1 – (KJV)*

Can you imagine the level of faith Jeremiah must have had in order to speak to people as a prophet at such a young age? Picture a child boldly telling adults what is going to happen in their lives without trepidation. I realize that in today's society some children are telling their parents what to do, but such was not the case back then. Jeremiah had to rely on God every step of the way through his faith in order to get the intended message across.

Now that God has revealed to you the call that He has on your life to achieve something greater, it's time you begin to practice the faith that is necessary to bring the greatness out of you. In other words, you need to believe that you can do all things through Christ who will give you the strength to accomplish what seems to be the impossible at the present time (Philippians 4:13). Faith is a critical component to achieving your goals because your goals almost always begin as an idea or vision, and because your aspirations are mere ideas during this stage, your faith is what will allow your visions and goals to manifest themselves for the world to see. For me, even as I write this, I am finding that I have to rely heavily on my faith in God in order to complete this chapter, much less the entire book, because I often have doubts as to whether I can accomplish such a task. Yes, the Lord told me to write this book and, yes, the Lord said that the book would bless people as a result. However, having never done anything like this before, I am terrified that I don't have it in me to get it done. But the resounding voice that I hear constantly while sitting at this computer is, *"I am with you."* You see, when the Lord gives you something to do, you need to have the assurance that He will not give you a vision for something, and then leave you to your own devices to get it done. The Lord issues a promise to us in Deuteronomy 31:6 to *"Be strong and of a good courage, fear not, nor be afraid of them: for the Lord thy God, He it is that doth go with thee; He will not fail thee, nor forsake thee."* The key thing to remember is not to let your fear overwhelm your faith. Sometimes as humans we fear the unknown. If we cannot see the end result of a particular thing, we'll most likely not pursue it. But fear is contrary to the will of God, and is nothing more than an illegitimate trick of the devil. II Timothy 1:7 validates my statements by declaring: *"For God hath not given us the spirit of fear; but of power, and of love, and of a sound mind."* Look at the key text for this chapter again. Hebrews 11:1 says that faith is the substance of things *hoped* for. Let's look at the definition for the word substance for a moment to gain further insight. The very word substance means: *"the actual matter of a thing, as opposed to the appearance or shadow; reality."* So then by definition, if faith is the actual matter of a thing, faith, which the Bible declares is the evidence of things not seen, is what actually causes a vision to turn into a reality. In order for the greatness inside of you to be manifested, you'll need to exercise your faith.

The Bible further goes on to illustrate in Hebrews 11:6 that *"...without faith it is impossible to please Him..."* As we discussed in the previous chapter, seeking God should be your place of origin when pursuing your call to something greater. But more importantly, seeking to please God should be your ultimate goal in general. If God is not pleased with you while you are in your pursuits, then what is the point? You may rise to acclaim and prestige "on your own", but if you're not careful to acknowledge the presence of God that is with you, then you could find yourself operating in the position but lacking the necessary Power to sustain you along the way. Make no mistake about it; your faith is critical to bringing your call to greatness to fruition.

You may be asking yourself, *"What kind of faith should I possess?"* First, let's define the word faith. Faith is defined as, *1) confidence or trust in a person or thing; 2) belief that is not based on proof.* Given this definition, an interchangeable word for faith can be belief. Since the words faith and belief are linked, let's now answer the above question.

BELIEF IN GOD
In order for you to have faith, you must first believe in God. Hebrews 11:6 in its entirety reads: *"But without faith it is impossible to please Him: for he that cometh to God must first believe that He is, and that He is a rewarder of them that diligently seek Him."* Pause for a moment and ask yourself this question: *Who was the one that revealed to me what my call to something greater was?"* Another question you could ask is, *"How did I come to the realization that there was something special inside of me?* You see, in order for your special gift to manifest, you need to acknowledge that there is Someone greater than you revealing this information to you.

Some call it a conscience; some call it the Holy Spirit. However you choose to describe it, know that it did not come from you by yourself. It came from deep within you, and my personal conviction is that the Lord revealed to you His plan for your life. The Bible affirms my position by asserting the following in II Timothy 1:14, *"That good thing which was committed unto thee keep by the Holy Ghost which dwelleth in us."* Furthermore, Acts 17:28 decrees: *"For in Him we live, and move, and have our being..."* Since I choose to believe the aforementioned, the only logical thing for me to do in order to succeed in going after my destiny that awaits me is to believe in the God who gave me the vision for my destiny in the first place. And naturally, I would recommend that you maintain a similar thought pattern because remember, I am simply sharing with you what has and is currently working for me.

Your belief in God is also going to play a critical role during those times you are pursuing your vision and thoughts of doubt begin to emerge from seemingly out of nowhere. As I stated before, I am terrified of writing this book. However, since God told me to write it, technically, it isn't my book anyway—it belongs to God. Since this book is connected to God's will for my life, whenever I am unable to write because of writers block, or I begin to feel doubtful that I can even finish it, my faith (in this case my belief), kicks in and eradicates my doubt and causes me to persevere knowing that the King of Kings is in control over His vision for my life. You should have the same confidence. You'll be surprised at how much you'll rely on your belief in God while you are pursuing your greatness. Trust me, God will never disappoint you!

BELIEF IN YOURSELF
Another key area as it relates to faith is the belief you will need to have in yourself. It hurts me sometimes when I hear people speaking of the great things that they wish to accomplish, but when you hear them speak it sounds like they don't even believe in their own words. Some people will begin to speak great things over their lives but then begin to make excuses in the same sentence declaring all of the reasons why they cannot do what it is that their heart desires. The advice I would share is simply this: it is not fair to ask someone else to believe in you and what you wish to do if you refuse to believe in yourself. Sometimes, you need to become your own motivator. When you can't turn to a loved one, a friend, or anyone else you would normally look to for support, and you're seemingly left all alone with just your thoughts, it's your belief in yourself that will help you to keep persisting.

There are several ways you can build confidence in yourself. One of the ways I like to use is to set small goals for myself and then seek to accomplish those goals. To me, there is no greater confidence builder than to finish something. But the key is refusing to celebrate that accomplishment too long. So many people accomplish a specific task, celebrate the victory, which is necessary to do, but end up celebrating too long and they end up missing the point of the entire exercise. Celebrating is vital for your confidence but moving on to another challenge is more important. The reason behind this is that the more victories you have achieved, though small ones now, they will eventually lead to you achieving greater victories. And once you have developed a habit of not only starting something, but also finishing it, you'll soon discover that you have the confidence necessary to pursue any challenge you may face. This will also help when your mind tries to tell you that you cannot do a certain task. But because of your faithfulness with these other projects, you'll be able to remind yourself of all the hard work you put into accomplishing these other tasks, thus, enabling you to press forward.

CHAPTER RECAP

When it comes to pursuing your call to something greater, you will need to exercise your faith along the way. This faith must begin with God. God gave you the dreams, talent, and ability, so why leave Him behind? Take the Spirit of God with you in faith and you'll be able to move mountains! I'm not saying that your faith has to be of supernatural proportions in the beginning. As a matter of fact, there are times in my journey of walking in the destiny that God has called me to that my faith actually diminishes. Sometimes I have great faith, and other times not so much. But the Bible offers us words of encouragement in Matthew 17:20 where it says that "...if ye have faith as a grain of mustard seed, ye shall say unto this mountain, Remove hence to yonder place; and it shall remove; and nothing shall be impossible unto you."

It's ironic that Jesus used the mustard seed in his illustration, considering the mustard seed is one of the smallest seeds in existence. I don't know about you, but I marvel at the fact that my mustard seed faith can move a mountain. Imagine what my greater sized faith can do! The only way to develop great faith is to believe in God and to experience

Him daily. See to it that you exercise your faith daily and before you know it, you'll look up and discover that the power of God within you will have you doing the impossible!

This area is important too so don't miss it. You need to also believe in yourself every step of the way. Yes, you will doubt yourself along the way and, yes, you will want to give up. But remember, if you do not believe in yourself, don't expect anyone else to believe in you either. I would recommend setting small goals daily and then strive to accomplish those goals. After about a week's worth of accomplishing small tasks, your confidence will begin to build.

Keep going! You're now on your way to your call to something greater. If you give up now, you're just going to have to start all over again. I'm willing to believe in you because I know Whose power you have living inside of you. The real question is, do you believe in yourself?

> *"Faith is taking the first step even when you don't see the whole staircase.*
> *Martin Luther King, Jr*

GREATER>

CHAPTER 5
MENTAL TOUGHNESS

And be not conformed to this world: but be ye transformed by the renewing of your mind, that ye may prove what is that good, and acceptable, and perfect, will of God.
Romans 12:2 – (KJV)

Jeremiah was severely persecuted because of the messages he delivered. Make no mistake, a lot of this persecution was not just physical but mental as well. Not only was he rejected as a messenger, his message was also rejected. It's one thing to be rejected as a preacher, it's another thing altogether to have your message rejected also. If people don't like me as a person, that's fine. But don't reject the message that the Lord has given me. Any preacher will tell you that preaching a sermon is usually easier than the sermon preparation process. I'm not saying that every sermon will be a *"home run"* because it will not. But, the goal is for people to at least receive the message. This was not the case with Jeremiah. Jeremiah prophesied his heart out, only to have the words given to him by the Lord fall to the ground. This would be mentally tough on anyone. If it were me, I would have reexamined my call to ministry. I probably would have even asked God to give me another call that was not as mentally draining. But despite all of this, Jeremiah made the decision to keep the word of the Lord in his mouth at all times. He continued to preach God's words without hesitation.

Every journey to greatness begins with a decision. In other words, if your mind is not equipped to handle the journey that is ahead, you will likely never go anywhere. It is vital as you continue reading this book that you not merely gloss over this chapter, because doing so may possibly cause you to miss out on realizing the greatness that lies within you. Anyone who has ever done anything noteworthy will tell you that they have at one point or another on their journey to excellence had a battle raging in their minds. You see, your mind is a literal battlefield, and in order for the greatness that is inside of you to be realized, you need to have a strong mind. It is often said, *"the mind is the devils playground."* What this means is that the devil is always seeking to cloud your thought process and try to eliminate those thoughts that have you wanting to better yourself. Now is the time that I would admonish you to be closer to Christ than you have ever been because you will need His power to help you transform your mind. Let's examine this text more closely to see what principles we can glean from having a transformed mind.

First, we are not to be conformed to this world. Many of you have no doubt thought about various ways you are going to prosper once your call to something greater is manifested. There are some who may desire to purchase new homes, while others may wish to purchase new cars, or both! You may have dreams of paying off all your bills, traveling across the globe and staying in the most expensive hotels. Maybe you simply wish to stockpile all of your earnings into your bank accounts or IRAs so that you can retire in a grandiose fashion. While these plans of monetary success are OK to some extent, it is crucial for the Christian to not seek what the world defines as wealth. Yes, your financial security is within the will of God but not for the reasons the world thinks. The only reason God would bless His children with overflow is so they can take the overflow and pour it back into His kingdom by ministering to other people. God declares in the Bible that He wants us to be lenders and not borrowers. The only way that we are going to be able to lend to others is if we have increase. The Bible also states in Matthew 19:21: *"Jesus said unto him, If thou wilt be perfect, go and sell that thou hast, and give to the poor, and thou shalt have treasure in heaven:*

and come and follow me." This means that we should assist the poor with our riches if we are to follow God. Remember, if you are seeking to live out your call to something greater, it is necessary to seek God first.

The Bible is filled with other illustrations on the real meaning of wealth. The point is to not allow the world's point of view to get in the way of God's will for our lives. It is very easy to become consumed with making money to the point that we miss out on the truer blessings of God. The Bible illustrates, in Luke 12:16-21, a parable of a man who had so much wealth he destroyed the barns that he had and sought to build bigger barns. At no time did this wealthy man seek to give to the poor and needy. If you search the scriptures further, you'll notice that the poor had a special place in the heart of God. I'm not trying to insinuate that God does not desire for us to enjoy the wealth He gives us. I'm simply saying that God desires us to pour into the lives of others as well. Imagine how successful you are going to be. Then, imagine how much more successful those around you could be if you pour your blessings back into them. There's a saying that goes: *"If you give a man a fish, he'll eat for a day. But if you teach a man to fish, he'll eat for a lifetime."* I am a firm believer that before you teach a man to fish you need to give him a fish so that his hunger will not deter him from receiving the information you have to share with him. Yes, it is true that you should not enable a person by providing them with continual handouts. However, it's difficult for people to truly receive all the information you have for them if they are hungry, or without suitable clothing, or lacking in other areas. The world says keep your money to yourself but God sees it differently. I will conclude this point by expressing it another way, *provide a hand up not just a hand out.* Both are necessary if you are truly going to live the dreams that God has for your life.

SEEK THE MIND OF CHRIST
Next, the text admonishes us to be transformed by the renewing of our minds. I can truly attest to the fact that anytime you wish to change your circumstance for the better, your mind will play tricks on you along the way. These tricks can be in the form of doubt, fear, anxiety, and other fabrications that you should never allow to take root in your thoughts. I must warn you that these thoughts will come. However, the key to eradicating them as they occur is to dismiss them as foolish attempts from the devil. Before writing this chapter, I was encouraged by a verse found in Philippians 4:13 that states: *"I can do all things through Christ which strengthens me."* In

all honesty, repeating this verse when my mind is battling, the Spirit's desire always fixes the situation. That is why I have to be very cautious of what I allow my brain to partake of. If you are serious about obtaining greatness in Christ, you need to have the mind of Christ. Philippians 2:5 declares: *"Let this mind be in you, which was also in Christ Jesus."*

A person who is desirous of having the mind of Christ should be careful when allowing certain things to enter into their minds. It is often said that you get out of something what is first put into it. In other words, the things that enter your mind will most certainly come out in some way, shape or form.

THOUGHTS BECOME ACTIONS

Believe it or not, most of the things we think about eventually become actions. Reflect back on some of the things you have accomplished. You were able to get those things done because you said you would do them. No doubt those things first began with a thought. This is another reason why it is important to have the mind of Christ. One of our primary concerns with seeking to achieve something greater is to have our thoughts one with Christ's. If we would simply trust God and allow Him to control our minds we'd be better off. So often we allow the images we see in movies, television, video games, books and magazines, as well as other forms of entertainment to saturate our minds. Let me give you an example. How many times have you gone to see an action movie and leave the theater thinking you could do some of the stunts that were done in the movie? Maybe you imagined living a life similar to that of the main character in the movie. I know I have done that several times. This goes to show you how we need to be careful of what we allow to enter into our minds because, eventually, the will become actions. If you fill your mind with violence all day, chances are, you will sooner or later commit a violent act. But if you were to fill your mind with thoughts that were pure and holy, it's very likely that you will begin acting upon those thoughts and start to live a life that one would consider pure. The Bible speaks to this in Philippians 4:8 where is says: *"Finally, brethren, whatsoever things are true, whatsoever things are honest, whatsoever things are just, whatsoever things are pure, whatsoever things are lovely, whatsoever things are of good report; if there be any virtue, and if there be any praise, think on these things."* We often refer to the analogy *"you are what you eat."* I would like to phrase it another way to drive this point home: *"you are what you think."* Think like a winner, you'll become a winner. Think like a loser and don't be upset or surprised when you find yourself losing all the time.

CHAPTER RECAP

Think about a sports figure who has won a major championship. Do you think Michael Jordan ever thought to himself, *"I wonder what it would be like to intentionally lose a championship?"* Do you think anyone who has ever won an NBA title, a Super Bowl, or any other prestigious sports trophy went into that game thinking about losing? No! Even before they got to the championship game, which took quite a bit of focus and determination might I add, they started preparing their minds to win their championship far in advance. If you are to ever become successful in the things you have been called to do, you need to begin by changing your thoughts. I am a firm believer that your thoughts can either make you or break you. If you truly want to become what God wants you to be, then prepare for it by asking God to give you a new mind. I am willing to guarantee that you will not make it to the next level if you consistently focus on reasons why you can't get there. It is imperative that you begin this journey with the end in mind. In other words, think about where you would like to be next year. Once you begin to think about this and visualize being in a different position than where you currently are, let that be your driving force when it comes to acting upon those thoughts. If you want better, think better. When it comes to going after your call to something greater, the only way you can adjust your thought-pattern is to have Christ give you a new mind. So my question to you is this: *What are you thinking about?*

> *"Strength is the product of struggle"*
> **Unknown**

GREATER>

CHAPTER 6
TRANSITIONING TO YOUR GREATNESS

Have I not commanded thee? Be strong and of good courage; be not afraid, neither be thou dismayed: for the Lord thy God is with thee whithersoever thou goest.
Joshua 1:9 – (KJV)

According to scripture, Jeremiah didn't have much time to transition from where he was to where God wanted him to be. In fact, God told Jeremiah to, "...*therefore gird up thy loins, and arise, and speak unto them all that I command thee...*" Jeremiah was to immediately go and do what God told him to do.

Now that you have been given what I believe to be the foundation of achieving your call to something greater (that is, beginning your journey to the greatness that lies within you), in these next few chapters, I'd like to share a few principles that will help propel you into the greatness that God has for you. You've started with God, now you need to act upon what God is giving you. The Bible says in

James 2:17 that: *"Even so faith, if it hath not works, is dead, being alone."* In other words, God has given you a vision about your future and where He wants to take you. But it must not stop with just a vision or a dream. Unless you act upon this Heavenly wisdom, you will never see what God has for you. You can have all the faith in the world but if you never act on it, you will never be satisfied with yourself. I call this *faith-filled action*, as this is what separates most of the successful people I know from everyone else.

BE ON THE MOVE

One of the things that frustrates me the most is hearing people tell me that they want to receive the blessings that God has for them, yet when I ask them what they are doing about it, they often reply, *"nothing yet."* How is it that you desire something different but you haven't done anything different. Now in defense of some of these individuals, a lack of resources is hindering them from moving to the next level. I can attest to that fact because it has happened to me. However, lack of resources should never fully hinder you from moving out on faith in the direction of your goals. Remember, if you begin your journey to greatness with God, He is your source. So many of us are looking for a *resource*, when we neglect the fact that God is our original *Source!* He is not a refurbished, regenerated, or a renovated source. He is the main source and if God told you to do something, He is the One that will provide the resources to get that thing done. It is often said, *"God will provide provision for the vision."* Bottom line, once God has revealed to you what your greater calling is, rest assured that He will also reveal to you the finances necessary to bring it to pass.

In the sport of basketball, it is often taught by coaches that a player needs to learn how to move without the ball. In other words, in order for an offensive play to fully develop, players without the ball in their hands need to constantly move so that they can find themselves in the right position to receive a pass and possibly score a basket. Staying in one spot can cause the entire play to break down, thus causing a turnover. Too many turnovers have taken place in the lives of individuals who are not operating in the place that God has for them because they refuse to be on the move. Some people refuse to move because they are afraid. Others refuse to move because they are content with being where they are. But think about this concept for a moment. If you are in need of a job and you never put in any applications, how then can you expect to get hired? If you know that you need to lose weight but you never begin an exercise regimen or even begin to eat healthier foods, don't complain that you aren't getting the results you desire.

DON'T SPEAK ABOUT IT; BE ABOUT IT.
Many people speak positive thoughts concerning their future but they often stop there. If you really desire success, you need to implement what you speak. If you don't know where to begin, here are a few steps that I would recommend:

MAKE NOTE OF ALL YOUR GOALS AND IDEAS
Notating the things that God reveals to you will help you in your planning. You will discover that many times the Holy Spirit will implant ideas in your mind, but you may have a lot going on at the same time. So, keeping notes will prevent you from forgetting. It would also be helpful for you to carry around a recording device for audio notes. I know it seems old school, but I have found this to be really helpful for me when I need to remember something later on. The best part is you may not need to go out and buy a recording device since most modern cell phones have this feature already built in. So you should already have the tools you need. Whenever you get an idea simply write it down in your notebook or press the record button. This way, you'll be able to refer to it later on without having to try to remember what you were thinking.

SET DEADLINES FOR YOURSELF

As I stated earlier, it is imperative to just sit and dream about your future. However, if all it amounts to is a dream without action you'll never be fulfilled or satisfied with where you are. Once you have an idea as to where you would like to be, set a deadline for each idea. I would recommend setting daily goals. A friend of mine gave me advice relating to the process I should take while writing this book. The steps that he gave me were as follows:

- Write down your vision for each day early in the morning. Flush them all out to the point where you cannot think of anything else. *(This also highlights the point I made earlier in the book to strive to be an early riser. Spend time with God first, and then seek Him for wisdom as it relates to the rest of your day.)*
- Once everything has been written down, spend the rest of your day trying to accomplish those "agenda" items.
- At the close of your day; maybe an hour before your work day comes to an end, on the way home from work, before your family / recreational time in the evening, or even before you go to bed, reflect on what you were able to accomplish that day. Compare what you accomplished that day to your list you created earlier.

Once you have created and accomplished some of these daily goals, now you can try setting weekly and monthly goals. Again, I stress setting daily goals first so as to get smaller victories under your belt. The small victories should create momentum for you to obtain larger victories. Too often, people set large goals and deadlines only to fall short because they set out to do too much at one time. If you can manage setting large goals then, by all means, move forward. But if you know you have problems in this area, start small. The Bible says in Zechariah 4:10: *"For who hath despised the day of small things...?"* In other words, don't be discouraged if you're not yet doing all the things you would like to do. God says in Matthew 25:21 that if you have *"...been faithful over a few things, I will make thee ruler over many things..."* Once you have been faithful over the daily goals, God will allow you to tackle larger ones.

These steps should allow you to stay focused and on track while pursuing your dreams. For me, I used to think about so many different things and then try to accomplish them all at the same time. But I soon found out that I was either burned out from doing too much, or I was frustrated because I wasn't able to accomplish much of anything since my energy was scattered all over the place. While multi-tasking is essential, too much of it can cause unnecessary stress, leaving you depleted and can also cause you to doubt yourself which is contrary to your overall success.

START STRONG

Most people would subscribe to the following statement: *"It's not how you start, but how you finish."* While I agree with this to some extent, it's not entirely true. Think about most people who begin a New Year's resolution to join a gym. They start very strong for a couple of weeks or, in some cases, months but then they fall off soon after they begin. I don't want to focus on the fact that they didn't follow through. For now, let's look at how they started. They started with such zeal and passion—the same zeal and passion that was necessary for them to finish. But many people don't follow through because at the beginning they set a goal, and when they don't see the results they wanted, they allow themselves to fall short or give up altogether.

Any track and field runner will tell you that if you don't get a strong start off the blocks, it will be very difficult for you to win the race. Starting strong will allow you to finish stronger. While I don't mind in certain instances rooting for the underdog, no one should aim to be a consistent underdog. Starting strong will give you the necessary motivation to continue strong. Better yet, finish even stronger.

Another way to help you start strong is to determine why you are doing what you are doing. What motivates you? Why are you pursuing these dreams and goals? I would suggest writing these questions down with their in-depth answers and once you have done this, refer to it every day. If making the world better is your motivation, think about that each day. If being financially secure is your focus, then keep that at the forefront of your mind whenever you greet each day. One of the things I hope this book accomplishes is that it will propel people into the greatness that God has for them. The way I see it, if more people were operating in the call that God has for them, the better off we would be as a society. So whenever I want to slack off and not write, I have to remember all the people who need this book. I'm sure there are other books out there like this one, but since God told me to write it I believe this will be one of the books that will enrich lives like never before. That's part of my motivation. What's yours?

CHAPTER RECAP

In transitioning to your greatness, you need to now shift your focus from leaving where you are and beginning the journey to where you want to be. If you wanted to take a road trip, how can you get to your desired destination if you never get in the car? But getting in the car is not enough. You need to actually put it in gear and start driving. Too many people settle for getting in the car but they never actually drive it. Your dream is like an exotic car. It may look good on the showroom floor, but if you never get behind the wheel and take it for a drive that car is not serving its purpose. A car was meant to be driven! So it is with your dream. It was not meant to remain a dream, but to be lived in reality. Why settle for just dreaming about something? Go get it! Ask God to give you new dreams. Once you have those dreams, write them down so you can go back to them when needed. Then, set deadlines to attack these dreams. You must also remember that you need to start strong. If you do these things, your transition will be underway and soon you'll be walking in your call to something greater!

"Today I will do the things that other people won't, so tomorrow I can do the things that other people can't" - Unknown

GREATER >

CHAPTER 7
CRITICISM FROM OTHERS

But the natural man receiveth not the things of the Spirit of God: for they are foolishness unto him: neither can he know them, because they are spiritually discerned.
1 Corinthians 2:14 (KJV)

Please understand that whenever you pursue something that is worth anything, unfortunately, there will always be someone who is ready to criticize you for it. If anyone knows this to be true, it's Jeremiah. Jeremiah was criticized by everyone including his family, friends, church members and generally anyone who didn't want to hear his message. The criticism that you will undoubtedly receive will come in various forms, but most often in the form of someone telling you how insufficient you are, reminding you of the skills that you do not possess, your lack of education, etc.

When this occurs most people allow it to derail them and they stop pursing their ambitions. However, this should never be used as an excuse to quit. Realize that, usually, when people criticize you, they are not necessarily attacking you and your dreams. More than likely, they are dissatisfied with themselves because they aren't walking in their greatness yet. Because they can't see themselves doing something great, they seek to tell others that they can't be great either. Don't allow someone else's failures to determine whether or not you will follow through on your dreams.

UNGODLY CRITICISM
Please keep in mind that there is no way you are going to please everyone. No matter how hard you try someone will always find something *wrong* with what you're doing. But if you have been implementing the principles outlined in this book, then you already know that the call that has been placed on your life to something greater didn't originate with you; God gave it to you. So since God gave you the dreams and desires, as long as you don't give up on them, the ungodly and discouraging criticism that you will undoubtedly encounter from others shouldn't matter to you. It may be hurtful but don't let it get you down. This is where you need to dig deep and press on regardless of what people may say along the way. The text I gave you - I Corinthians 2:14, basically tells us that not everyone is spiritually minded. And since they don't have the

Spirit guiding them, they are merely looking at the natural things like talent and ability. So the spiritual call on your life cannot be discerned by them. This is where the phrase, *"spiritual things are spiritually discerned"* comes from.

Psalm 1:1 further clarifies this point, *"Blessed is the man that walketh not in the counsel of the ungodly..."* Think about it; why would you listen to people who aren't living up to their God-ordained potential anyway? I find it rather funny when people try to advise you on how you should handle your business when they aren't handling their own business! However, this is not a time to shy away from your vision, nor is it a time to retaliate verbally to these individuals.

Many times, I have encountered this type of ungodly criticism from people and, admittedly, lashed out at these individuals verbally—which did more harm than good. You need to understand that sometimes these people are put in your path by the devil to get you off track. One of the most important things to remember while on this journey to something greater is that your character can make you or break you. I would even dare to say that if your character isn't acceptable to God, you may never realize your dreams. Am I saying that one has to be perfect before walking in their true calling? No, I am not. The grace and mercy of God is indescribable. What I'm saying is that even if you end up walking in your greater calling, but your character doesn't match up you've defeated the whole purpose.

The goal of walking in your calling is not just for you, it's also for others that you may bless along the way. No one will want to hear what you have to say if you have questionable character or a bad reputation. Hence, follow the plan detailed in this book by beginning with God so that He can build and refine your character as you proceed.

Also, keep in mind that doing what God has called you to do will often times attract haters! When these haters see someone else doing something positive in their lives, jealousy and resentment sets in. This can cause them to doubt you when you say you are going to do something. They may flatout trash your ideas and say you should be doing something else. What you need to do when this occurs is let it fuel you even more! Every time someone says something negative about your vision, use it as a motivational tool and work even harder to get it done.

While writing this book, there were several people

who doubted that I was capable of doing such a thing, and probably hoped I would fail. But instead of feeding into that nonsense, I had to make myself write. And let's not forget about those who the devil will *assign* to attack you. That's right! There are negative forces that the devil has employed to attack you while on this journey. But you have to think to yourself, *"since they are doing their jobs in attacking me, why shouldn't I continue doing my job in going after my call to something greater?"* These forces are hard at work, and if you allow them, they will distract you from your job.

Look at it this way: Since they do their jobs so well, why not do your job even better? I know some of you wish these haters would just miss you altogether and find someone else to hate on. But if you think about it, every successful person who has ever lived has faced a hater. If you want to be successful in life, embrace it, use it to motivate you, and then once you are living your dreams, you'll be able to declare that you endured in spite of the negativity. I do want to caution you, however, to not rub your success in the face of your haters. Them seeing you live out your success will do that for you. If you only want to be successful in order to get revenge on your haters, then you are missing the point of being successful in the first place. God says to us in Romans

12:19 to, "...*avenge not yourselves, but rather give place unto wrath: for it is written, Vengeance is mine; I will repay, saith the Lord.*" Let God handle your revenge. Would you rather get revenge on somebody or God get revenge on somebody for you? Again, when seeking to live out the purpose that God has for you, make sure your character lines up with God's call on your life. God doesn't want you taking matters into your own hands. He wants you to trust Him to fight your battles for you. If you understand the concept found in II Chronicles 20:15, which says, "*...for the battle is not yours, but God's,*" then you'll truly become successful while living your true calling.

GODLY CRITICISM

The other type of criticism that you will encounter during this transition is constructive criticism. Unlike ungodly criticism, constructive criticism is vital to anyone who is desirous of becoming successful. You need this kind of criticism in order to persevere. God will sometimes send people your way to give you advice on where you are, and also on how to proceed. Remember, since spiritual things are spiritually discerned, and you are, in fact, living in the Spirit, God will send you other spiritually minded people to help you along the way. It is important not to view their advice as you would those who are presenting ungodly criticism because you could end up missing out on a tremendous blessing. Psalm 141:5 instructs, *"Let the righteous smite me; it shall be a kindness: and let him reprove me; it shall be an excellent oil, which shall not break my head: for yet my prayer also shall be in their calamities."* So just to reiterate, you need godly criticism.

Please understand that every decision you make during this transition will not be a good one. If you are opposed to constructive criticism, then how will you be able to handle or even reach the level of success that God is calling you to? Think for a moment about any company you see in operation today. Do you think they reached the level of success they are currently operating in without constructive criticism? Some companies have even gone so far as to place comment cards in their lobbies or on their websites *inviting* this type of criticism. Sure, they'll need to weed out the good comments from the bad ones but the point is that in order to be better you will need the advice of people who can help you become better. If these companies were to close their doors each time they received constructive criticism there wouldn't be any businesses open today.

Only people who think they know it all believe they don't need advice from anyone. Don't you just hate it when you run into someone who professes to know it all? Don't be the person you don't like. If you allow your pride to get in the way, you will only be delaying your success. If you're anything like me, you cannot afford any more self-appointed delays. Godly delays, sure. Self-appointed ones, not at all! I'm going to share with you a concept that we discuss on the prayer line. Imagine a diamond for a moment. Before you even get to see a diamond publicly they must first go through a cutting process in private. This is addressed to those of you whom God has given the opportunity to constructively criticize a person. Always do it privately, never publicly. It's important that the person cutting the diamond be qualified to cut and handle precious gemstones. If the diamond is cut too much it will be ruined. If the diamond is cut too little it typically won't have the shine or sparkle you expect to see in a diamond. You are this diamond, and in order for you to shine brightly, you need to have someone carefully and constructively cut you so that when others see you operating in your greatness, they will immediately see your worth.

Bear in mind, the point of receiving constructive criticism is to help you improve yourself or your ideas. An example of this is found in Exodus 18:14-18, where Moses' father-in-law, Jethro, gave him some constructive or godly criticism. Moses was tasked with hearing the judicial cases for the children of Israel. Because there were so many tribes, Moses was wearing himself out day after day attending to these matters. When Jethro came into town to visit, he noticed that Moses was stressed out because of how he was handling business. He proceeded to tell Moses that what he was doing was not good. Jethro told Moses that in order to prevent burnout he would need to delegate some of his judicial responsibilities to other capable men in the camp. Moses followed the wisdom given by his father-in-law, which resulted in a smoother operation that God was pleased with.

Notice a few important things here. First, Jethro did not stop by simply telling Moses all of the things that he was doing wrong. Often times, when people are giving what they perceive to be godly advice, they end up merely complaining about what is taking place rather than coming up with solutions on how to make the situation better. I always say if you're going to complain about something, come up with a solution to fix the problem. No one wants to hear a complainer all of the time. Instead, curtail your advice to not only include the problem but also a way to fix the problem.

Secondly, keeping what I just said in mind, Jethro gave Moses a solution that actually made sense. You can come up with a solution for a problem but make sure it is viable. If not, you may be doing more harm than good.

Thirdly, after you receive a practical solution to the problem, make sure you implement the solution only with God's permission. Jethro said to Moses in verse number 23 of Exodus 18 that, *"If thou shalt do this thing, and God command thee so, then thou shalt be able to endure..."* Jethro knew that Moses had a very close relationship with God and as a result, he did not want Moses to jeopardize that relationship by doing something out of God's will. The same should go for you when you receive advice from someone. No matter how godly a person is, always go back to God and seek His face to see if the advice that someone is giving you is in fact from the Lord. Not doing so could cause you to find yourself out of the will of God. I don't care if they are your Pastor or other spiritual leader. This is in no way meant to disrespect these individuals in your life. Yes, God may have sent them. But always consult with God to make sure their advice was really from God.

CHAPTER RECAP

Remember these few points I'm about to share with you and, if you do, you'll be that much farther ahead while pursuing your call to something greater!

NOT EVERYONE WILL SUPPORT YOUR CALLING
God specifically gave you the dreams, visions, and the special calling for your life. Because He gave it to you only, don't expect everyone to understand where you're coming from. I know you are excited to tell others what God is getting ready to do in your life. I know because I was, and still am to a certain extent, the same way.

KEEP CERTAIN DETAILS ABOUT YOUR CALLING PRIVATE
I would also recommend keeping certain details of your unique calling a secret until God fully manifests them in you. Some people don't need to know everything about your calling because by telling them everything, you are actually giving them fuel to criticize you. In other words, let certain people see you already operating in your God-given greatness. People will still hate on you but you'll be living your dreams, and that alone should give you some extra confidence to disregard any negativity concerning you and your calling.

DON'T LASH OUT AT SOMEONE BECAUSE THEY HATE ON YOU

It will be very tempting to verbally attack someone for some of the hurtful things they may say about your calling. This is where you need to exercise love and view this as the Holy Spirit trying to perfect your character. Remember, having a godly character is of the utmost importance if you are truly going to live your call to something greater.

USE THIS NEGATIVITY TO YOUR ADVANTAGE

Since it's clear that you cannot avoid ungodly criticism, use it as fuel to get to the next level. But be careful here! Once you make it to the next level, don't throw your success in the faces of those who didn't believe in you. Your success will do that by itself and God will see to it. Let God fight your battles on your behalf. As long as you stay focused on what you need to do, God will take care of the rest.

GODLY CRITICISM IS NECESSARY

Psalm 37:23 says, *"The steps of a good man are ordered by the Lord…"* Since your steps have already been orchestrated by God, this means that He has already carefully identified individuals to come your way with positive advice on their tongues. Don't reject their criticism. Doing so could lead you to rejecting the voice of God.

DON'T ALLOW YOUR PRIDE TO HINDER YOUR BLESSINGS
I come across people all the time who think they know it all. Don't be like these people. When someone gives you advice, pray about it, and if God gives you permission to implement it, then proceed to do so. Not everyone is out to hurt you.

CRITICIZE IN A MANNER PLEASING TO CHRIST
If God has placed you into someone's life to be an asset to him or her by offering constructive criticism, do so in a manner that God will approve of. Not doing so could be severely detrimental to the person to whom you are providing the advice. Also, give your criticisms in private, never in public. Your advice is meant to better the person, so there is no need for other people to hear what you're saying.

YOU ARE A DIAMOND; SHINE LIKE ONE
In order for you to shine brightly like a diamond does, it is necessary for you to first go through a cutting phase. Once qualified individuals have cut you properly, then you will be ready to fully display your true calling for the world to see. It is then that others will be able to see your true value.

> *"Keep away from people who try to belittle your ambitions. Small people always do that, but the really great make you feel that you, too, can become great."*
> *- Mark Twain*

‹GREATER›

>

CHAPTER 8
SUPPORT SYSTEM

*Wherefore comfort yourselves together,
and edify one another, even as also ye do.*
1 Thessalonians 5:11– (KJV)

Maintaining peace and harmony when receiving various types of criticism, it is important. Remember that whenever you start something as noteworthy as pursuing your call to something greater, it's always necessary to have someone in your corner pushing you to achieve whatever your goals are. Regardless of how many people discourage you, you'll need at least one person in your corner who believes in you. As it relates to Jeremiah, it's sort of difficult to find supporters of his ministry because Jeremiah preached about matters of judgment that often alienated people. The people in Jeremiah's day were similar to people in our day. When people are doing wrong, they rarely want to be told of their wrong doing, much less hear of the consequences that will result from their wrong doing. There were a few people, however, that supported Jeremiah. Their support came in the form of their obedience to the words God had given Jeremiah.

Consider it this way: Whenever you go to the gym, while you can get an effective workout on your own, you will typically achieve better results if you go with a workout partner. I must admit if I don't have a workout partner, I rarely go to the gym. The reason for this is because having a workout partner causes you to limit your rest in between sets and, also, it allows the workout to move at a faster pace. Someone encouraging you to go hard on one more rep, one more set, or one more routine gives you more drive. Let's not forget about the safety benefits either. For example, when bench pressing, it is highly advised that you have someone behind you spotting you in the event that something happens and you can't get the weight off you. These are just a few reasons why having a support system is beneficial to you. Here are some tips to remember concerning your support system.

WHO ARE YOU SUPPORTING?
Before identifying people who are in your support system I'd like to interject a concept, and if you follow it, it will allow you to go much farther on your journey. Instead of always trying to find people to help you, first ask yourself who are you willing to help? Too many people want help but they themselves aren't willing to help anyone else. I have found that the more you give of yourself, the more God will give back to you in return. In case you

haven't figured this out by now, I won't give you a principle without giving you some scripture to substantiate what I am saying. Luke 6:38 gives a perfect example of pouring into others where it admonishes, *"Give, and it shall be given unto you; good measure, pressed down, and shaken together, and running over..."* Most people try to use this text to support financial gain. However, if you inspect the text more closely, it is not referring to financial prosperity per se, rather, it's referring to how much love you give to an individual. It's similar to the principle of sowing and reaping. Whatever you plant into the ground is what you will reap. If you plant orange seeds, don't expect an apple tree. In other words, if you sow support for others, you'll reap support from others. If you sow hate and contempt, you'll reap the same thing. So now the question becomes, what is it that you really want? Do you want love? Then you'll need to give love first.

SUPPORT SELFLESSLY

Once you have made the decision to support others, make sure you do it out of a pure spirit. Don't support others just so you can get something in return. Yes, the promise in Luke 6:38 assures you that you will reap what you sow, but if you sow only for your gain, then you've missed the point. Let's go back to planting seeds for moment. If you were to plant the seeds of an orange tree it would be correct to expect an orange tree in return. However, what are you going to do with the fruit of that tree? Are you just going to hoard it all for yourself, or are you going to allow others to partake of the fruit? When you pour into others, it's not just for your benefit; it should also be for the benefit of others. When you discover the art of putting other people's needs above your own, that's when you'll discover a call to something greater that is unlike any other.

PEOPLE YOU CAN TRUST
No one should want someone in their circle who will not be honest with them. More so, no one wants to be in your circle if they fear that you will not be honest with them. Being trustworthy goes a long way in any industry, and whatever God is calling you to, you need to make sure that not only can you trust others but they can trust you as well. Refusing to trust others can be viewed as you willingly choosing to isolate yourself. Refusing to connect with people causes you to not have anyone in your corner when you need them most. Trust me when I tell you that when you are on a journey to something greater, this will be a time like never before, and you'll need to have someone in your corner that you can talk to at any time—especially when times get rough.

As I stated earlier, make sure that the people in your corner can be trusted. Not just from a truth or lie perspective, but rather, you'll want to make sure that you can trust the advice they will give you. You don't just want a bunch of "yes-men" in your corner. Make sure these people have your best interest at heart and only desire the best for you and your success.

WATCH WHO YOU SURROUND YOURSELF WITH
You'll also need to be especially mindful of who you surround yourself with. Would you want people who are unethical in your corner? I would hope not. Am I saying that you should avoid these people at all cost? Well, maybe. There are some people you need to avoid altogether. For instance, there are people I know who used to be friends of mine but I know they don't have my best interest at heart. It wouldn't be wise for me to continue hanging with them while pursuing the things that God has for me. However, you can still be a witness to these individuals. The Bible says in 1 Peter 3:16: *"Having a good conscience; that, whereas they speak evil of you, as of evildoers, they may be ashamed that falsely accuse your good conversation in Christ."* A passage that is commonly used to paraphrase this text is, *"don't let your good be evil spoken of."* Sure you can be a witness, just don't let your witness cause you to revert back to old habits and patterns that don't match up with your calling.

CHAPTER RECAP

Having a healthy support system is so important during your transition that I would go so far as to say that if you don't have one, you aren't going to be as successful as you'd like. Yes, it's true that if God is for you then who can be against you (Romans 8:31). However, God never intended for you to be an island all to yourself. He desires that you develop healthy relationships with others so that you can encourage one another and build each other up.

Look at a boxer. A boxer always has someone in their corner that they can trust to encourage them while they fight. While you are in the ring fighting for your dreams, you need to make sure that you have someone in your corner to motivate you to continue on until the fight is over.

Also, remember that just how you want and need someone in your corner, someone needs you to be in his or her corner as well. Find someone to mentor and pour into along this journey. I guarantee that God will reward you richly for it.

> *"Encourage, lift and strengthen one another. For the positive energy spread to one will be felt by us all.*
> *For we are connected, one and all."*
> *- Deborah Day*

SUPPORT SYSTEM

DARRELL A. PALMES III

GREATER>

CHAPTER 9
LOOKING THE PART

Put on the whole armour of God, that ye may be able to stand against the wiles of the devil.
Ephesians 6:11– (KJV)

In Jeremiah 29, God instructs Jeremiah to tell the people to look the part; to have an appearance based not only upon where they were but where they would be someday. The children of Israel were commanded to build houses, marry, have children, and act as if everything was normal even though they were in captivity. If they did not begin to look the part in their present state, their future could have been severely compromised.

It is important for you to realize, whether you like it or not, that whatever the greatness is God has called you to, it will require you to change your appearance to aptly befit your calling. This can range from changing the way you dress to changing the way you speak or even act. While it is true that 1 Samuel 16:7 says, "*...for man looketh on the outward appearance, but the Lord looketh on the heart,*" it is important to make sure that your outward matches up with your inward. Whether right or wrong, perception is reality. Here are a few points that will help you to understand what I'm saying.

MODIFY YOUR APPEARANCE
Relax! I'm not talking about plastic surgery or anything that drastic. Rather, I'm referring to the clothes you wear. Imagine seeing a police officer on the street. I'm not talking about an undercover officer, I mean a uniformed officer. You can immediately spot an officer based on his or her attire. Their uniform matches their position. The same goes for a fireman. When you see a fireman responding to a fire they don't show up dressed any way they want. In order to successfully fight that fire, they need to have on the proper attire. Still don't follow me? No problem. Think back to every time you have seen the President of the United States of America on television. Very rarely will you see the President dress in anything other than a suit and tie. Why? Because his position mandates that he look *"presidential."* Even if you were to catch a glimpse of the President on vacation with his family, he is still very well dressed. Image how you would feel if you were to see the President wearing baggy jeans and sneakers around the White House. I don't know about you, but I can just imagine the press he would receive for not looking the part. If the President would catch heat for dressing in anything less than his po-

sition directs, why shouldn't you or I catch the same heat?

Please don't bother using the excuse that neither of us are the President. After all, the whole point of this book is for you to walk in your true calling. If God were to tell you that you are going to be a future President of the United States of America, whether you are male or female, your preparation process would have to begin now. Presidents are not groomed to be Presidential overnight. They go through an extensive preparation process, and part of that process is to make sure they look the part of a *future* United States President. Notice I said *future*. You cannot wait until you get the job to change. Begin changing the way you dress now so that once you do begin walking in your calling, your way of dress is second nature to you. If you need helpful information on how to dress the part, keep reading. If you feel that you are already dressing the part and don't need any additional help in this area, continue to read so you can pass this information along to someone else. Remember, you reap what you sow.

MEN

CLOTHING – Instead of wearing loose fitting t-shirts all the time, invest in a few long-sleeve, button-up dress shirts. Whether you wear it out of your pants or inside, this alone will drastically change your appearance, especially if people are accustomed to seeing you in t-shirts all the time. Also, instead of baggy jeans and sneakers, invest in some dress slacks and a nice looking pair of dress shoes. You don't need to break the bank on your wardrobe here. Find a nice inexpensive store in your area that will help you facilitate this wardrobe change. Trust me, once you start implementing these principles, you'll soon make enough money to buy more expensive items. Lastly, when going to a job interview or any other business meeting, always dress in a suit, unless it was explicitly told to you beforehand not to wear one by the individuals you are meeting with. Believe it or not, this shows that you not only care about your appearance, but also that you care about how your job performance is viewed. Again, no need to spend a lot of money on a suit. Just make sure that the suit fits you properly by having it professionally tailored.

HAIR AND NAILS – I know this should go without saying, but please make sure that your hair and nails are professionally groomed when presenting yourself to others. When God called me to ministry, I had dreadlocks. While I didn't believe that this would hinder me from preaching in churches, a pastor once said to me that I would increase my chances of being taken seriously if I were to cut my hair. Now I am not suggesting that you go out and cut your hair, but I am suggesting that you need to be mindful of the visual presentation you make to others while on your journey to something greater. Regardless of your hairstyle, just make sure that it is always neat and presentable. Also, and don't laugh here, but you need to also make sure that there isn't any visible hair coming from your nose or ears. When trimming the hair on your head, make sure you don't forget the nose and ears as they are often easily overlooked. As for your nails, I know this is largely considered something that women take more pride in than we do. And rightly so. But look at it this way. Handshakes are customary among men. Unless you have been working on cars all day, why present your hand to another man and your nails are filthy? I know it doesn't seem like this should matter, but trust me, it does. It will go a long way if you remember to put your best self forward at all times.

WOMEN

Since I am not a woman, I cannot give you exact details here. But what I will say is that the same principles that apply to the men can in principle apply to you ladies. I will point out just a few things here as it relates to your appearance.

CLOTHING – Your clothes should fit you properly. There is never a situation in a professional environment that will call for you to wear tight fitting or revealing clothing. Never. Doing so will send the wrong message to people and will do more harm than good as it relates to you pursuing your call to something greater. Short skirts should be eliminated, in addition to cleavage-bearing tops. Yes, you may feel that the outfit looks good on you, and it may. However, keep in mind my previous words. You want to look the part of whatever God is calling you to. I refuse to believe that God is calling you to a greater level that warrants you having to wear a skirt that doesn't cover much or a top that shows most of your breasts. It's always best to let others see how smart you are not how good you look in a certain outfit.

HAIR AND NAILS – Much does not need to be said here, as most women usually do a good job of maintaining their hair and nails. I would caution, however, that having multiple vibrant colors in your hair doesn't look too good. In addition, having super long fingernails isn't a plus either. Neat and clean, short to medium length fingernails is usually the accepted norm. The same goes for nail colors. Contemporary colors are fine, but outlandish, vibrant colors should be deemed unacceptable.

Those were just a few bullet points concerning the outward appearance relating to looking the part. But have you considered any other areas of your *"appearance"* that can be modified to match the level of success that you are trying to reach?

MODIFY YOUR SPEECH
Similar to how your outward appearance is important, the way you verbally communicate is equally as important. If you're honest, you probably talk a certain way around your friends. You probably also speak a different way around your co-workers or your parents. If you're like me, sometimes you've let the two methods of communication mingle. This has either caused you to sound like you're trying to be someone else around your friends, or unprofessional to your co-workers. If this has been the case, I would simply recommend that you speak the same way all the time. Regardless of your environment, you can never go wrong by speaking in a clear and professional manner. Remember, you're trying to become better and achieve something greater. This means that you have to be willing to modify all aspects of yourself, if necessary. I'll leave it at that. Speak like you want to be spoken to. Always.

MODIFY YOUR ACTIONS
It is often said that, *"actions speak louder than*

words." You can speak about becoming a better person and pursuing your greatness all you want. But at some point you need to act upon what you say. This goes back to my earlier chapter about transitioning to your greatness. Think of it this way: What you do dictates what you receive in return. Act childish, expect childish results. Act like a failure, live in failure. But, if you act like a winner, you'll eventually become a winner. Act successful, become successful. Your actions can dictate your future.

CHAPTER RECAP

Implementing the changes are merely what worked for me. I do want to caution you on a few of these suggestions however. First, when changing your appearance, think of getting an extreme makeover. This may not be necessary for you. I simply desire that you put forth your best effort in looking good.

When it comes to your clothing, simply try to look the part of those you'll be around. For example, if I'm preaching at a youth event, I'm not wearing a suit and tie. I may wear a button-up, some jeans and some sneakers, or I may even wear a t-shirt and jeans with sneakers. But please know that I'm going to look presentable. This is what I want for you as well.

When speaking at a leadership conference, I'll put on a suit. It all depends on where I'm going. Don't necessarily *overdress*, but don't *underdress* either. Think of it this way: You are aiming for success.

The reality is that you only get one opportunity to make a first impression. You cannot afford to miss any more opportunities in your life right now. You're too close to your call to something greater! The way you look can either accelerate you to your greatness, or it can slow you down. Therefore, make sure that your entire presentation shows that you are ready for, and that you mean, business.

"You only get one chance to make a first impression."
Author Unknown

LOOKING THE PART

DARRELL A. PALMES III

<GREATER>

CHAPTER 10
PROCRASTINATION

*The hand of the diligent will rule,
but the lazy man will be put to forced labor.
Proverbs 12:24 — (NKJV)*

Jeremiah's entire life was lived without procrastination. Even though the message he preached was a difficult one, he still went about it. In other words, he was always moving about the business of the Lord. Even when he was in prison, he was still preaching what the Lord told him to preach. Yes, he was discouraged. Yes, he was often in despair. It's also true that he even battled with depression at times. But he never allowed himself to sit on what God told him to do. He always acted without delay.

If I can be honest, I am afraid to write this chapter because this is something that I struggle with greatly. God will give me an idea and depending on what it is, I'll sit on the idea. You must recognize that in order to reach your full potential, you are going to need to not sit on what God has given you to do.

ARE YOU THE HOLDUP?
People often ask why they haven't realized their

dreams yet. But when I in turn ask them if they have started on their dreams, they'll say 'not really.' Sometimes they say they don't know where to start. I refuse to accept this because there's a tool called the Internet. With the Internet, your favorite search engine can instantly bring up steps you can take to get things done. Whatever your goal, just type it in and someone has already listed steps for you to take to achieve it. The question is, how bad do you want it? No one can start this journey for you, you have to start it yourself. Once you begin, the Lord will send people your way to help you.

This is why I like to always be on the move. I like to actively seek new opportunities to present the message that God has given me. The only way people are going to give me an opportunity is if they see me. Using the analogy of basketball again, the best scorers are the ones that know how to move without the ball. The point guard won't pass you the ball if you are always standing in the same spot. Therefore, you need to always move. God is the point guard. Make sure that you are always in the spot, and He'll pass you the ball. And check this out—God being the point guard will often tell you where the spot is that you need to be in to receive the pass!

Many times God will tell me to go somewhere or do

something and for the life of me I don't understand why. But when I get to the place He wanted me to be, He either blesses me tremendously or allows me to bless someone else tremendously. Technically, I feel blessed just to help someone else out, so I end up receiving a blessing regardless. The point is, in order to get to the spot, you need to move. Don't say you're going to be at the spot and don't end up there. This can cause a turnover. Someone else can receive the pass that you were supposed to receive. This may result in them scoring points that should have been yours.

Recognize that just because God gave you a vision for something greater and you sat on it doesn't mean that He won't give that idea to someone else to achieve. There's not a worse feeling in the world than to see someone else out there walking in the anointing and purpose that was supposed to be yours. While they cannot do it like you because remember only you can do what you do, they sure can operate with *your* dream and idea with *their* swag (charisma)! Don't be the holdup to your breakthrough. A divine delay by the Lord... I'm cool with that. But don't cause your own delays.

Another analogy that can be used is missing an airline flight. I'm okay more or less missing a flight because of an airline delay. I'm not okay with missing a flight because I was late getting to the airport. The plane is going to leave. The question is, are you going to be on it?

Reasons People Procrastinate

FEAR OF SUCCESS
Many people don't pursue their dreams fully because of fear. I just refuse to accept this as a valid excuse for not pursuing your call. Here are some ways that I've seen people exhibit their fear of success:
- You feel guilty about your success because others around you don't have the same success
- You don't allow your ideas to be heard in a group setting because you want to avoid conflict with your co-workers, family, or friends. In other words, you go along with everyone else even though you have your own idea.
- You feel that you don't deserve success for whatever reason
- You feel that you won't be able to maintain the success, so you never even start so as not to let yourself or others down.

Don't get me wrong, these feelings may be valid but I would caution you here not to allow your feelings to dictate your future. Here are some ways I would recommend overcoming your fear of success. Ask yourself the following questions:

- What good could come from my success?
- What bad could come from my success?
- How will I feel a year from now if I still haven't started working on my dreams?
- How often do I visualize myself fulfilling my purpose in life?

If you ask yourself these questions, they should motivate you to press ahead. I would challenge you to use your fear of success as a motivational tool to get you moving forward. Once you become successful, I can guarantee you that most, if not all, of those fears will subside because of the very success you were afraid of in the beginning!

FEAR OF FAILURE

There are countless people who suffer from having a fear of failure. This may be one of the main reasons why people don't pursue their dreams. Some of the reasons people fear failure could be:

- They had a humiliating experience as a child in a certain area and they've vowed never to *"fail"* again in those areas now that they are adults.

- They associate the task at hand with a competition and fear they might not *"win."*

Again, I am not downplaying these fears. As a matter of fact, as I write this book, I am having doubts that it will connect with readers on all levels. If you are going to engage in anything worthwhile, failure is going to be a part of your journey at some point. You are going to hear more no's than yes'. The key, however, is to not let the "no's" of life discourage you. If and when you do fall, it's important to get back up again. The old saying *"if at first you don't succeed, try, try again"* has never been truer. Yes, your temporary failure is discouraging. But it would be more discouraging if you fail to continue working hard until you achieve your desired results.

For me, I know that God has called me to something greater. Since I know that I am called, God is the One who will handle the results. I may be a failure in someone else's opinion of me. But since I know that God has my back, failure is not an option. As the song writer said, *"There Is No Failure in God!"* The way to make this saying true is to keep pressing no matter what.

One way I would suggest overcoming your fear of failure is to write down exactly what you are afraid of on a sheet of paper. On that same sheet of paper, write down your desires. Once you have both lists, write out what would be the results if you were to allow your fear to hinder you from being successful. Then, write out what the possible outcomes would be if you were to actually success. Your results should motivate you to continue pressing forward. To put it plainly, at some point, you're going to have to turn the night light off and just go to sleep. Just remember, you can do all things through Christ who will give you the strength (Philippians 4:13).

FEAR OF SOMETHING NEW
This could also be referred to as the fear of change. Most people do not like to veer off the beaten path. They like to stay with what is familiar. Moving away from the predictable usually causes an uncomfortable feeling that overwhelms the person affected by this type of fear. Allow me to share a saying with you that, *"you cannot become successful until you become uncomfortable with being comfortable."* Being comfortable with your situation can often lead to laziness and a lack of motivation to pursue a higher level.

Let me give you an example. Most people have the idea that if they work a 9 to 5 job long enough, they'll eventually get the job they want. Once they arrive at that position, they feel like they'll be able to do all the things they've wanted to do in life. If this is you, have you paused to consider that the very motivation it took for you to get to that level is the same motivation you will need to maintain that level? In other words, the goal is to never be stagnant. In order to become truly successful, one must always be on the move, looking for new opportunities and areas in which to grow.

Even if you are in a state where you are "actively waiting" for the Lord to reveal to you what your next move should be, always seek to learn new things. If you're going to learn how to swim, you're eventually going to have to step away from the shallow waters and venture into the deeper waters. It is in the deeper waters that you develop a certain level of stamina like no other. Once you've mastered one level, it just makes sense to move on to another level.

CHAPTER RECAP

There is a common acronym for fear. F.E.A.R. is often referred to as *False Evidence Appearing Real*. Remember, God is on your side! This means that you can accomplish anything your heart desires. Although there are many different types of fear, the reality is that fear is not of God. Since you are now operating under kingdom principles, all fear must be evicted upon entry into your mind. Fear can cause you to forfeit God's greatest blessings for you. You have a choice to make. Either listen to the voice of fear telling you why you can't do something, or you can listen to the Voice of God and walk into the destiny that He has for you. Choose wisely.

For the remainder of this recap, I thought it fitting to use a few more quotes about procrastination to further illustrate my point. Take from them what you will. If I were you, I would use them to motivate me to start now. But rest assured, if you delay starting your dream, you'll delay accomplishing your dream.

"My advice is to never do tomorrow what you can do today. Procrastination is the thief of time."
– Charles Dickens

"Someday is not a day of the week."
— Janet Dailey

"God has promised forgiveness to your repentance, but He has not promised tomorrow to your procrastination."
— Saint Augustine of Hippo

"Only put off until tomorrow what you are willing to die having left undone."
— Pablo Picasso

"You may delay, but time will not."
— Benjamin Franklin

"A year from now you may wish you had started today."
— Karen Lamb

"You cannot escape the responsibility of tomorrow by evading it today." — Abraham Lincoln

"Never put off for tomorrow, what you can do today."
— Thomas Jefferson

"We are so scared of being judged that we look for every excuse to procrastinate."
— Erica Jong

> "...the best possible way to prepare for tomorrow is to concentrate with all your intelligence, all your enthusiasm, on doing today's work superbly today. That is the only possible way you can prepare for the future."
> — Dale Carnegie

GREATER>

\>

CHAPTER 11
FINISH STRONG

*And Jesus said unto him, No one, having put his
hand to the plough, and looking back,
is fit for the kingdom of God.*
Luke 9:62 – (KJV)

Now that you've begun to implement these principles, it's vital that you finish what you start. If you read the entire story of Jeremiah, you'll discover that he exemplified this point. No matter how difficult the situation was that he faced, he always finished strong. When no one was listening to him, he finished. While in prison, he finished. When his life was threatened, he finished. Even without winning many converts, he still finished! Still keep in mind that Jeremiah was a mere youth at the time of his calling. Not only does that display his consistency, it also displays his determination to complete the task that God had for him.

Again, being honest, finishing strong is something that I have been guilty of not doing in the past as well. There are things that God has told me to do that I have started, but I have yet to complete.

Truth be told, there is no reason why those things still cannot be completed right now, I just haven't done them yet. I'm a bit of a perfectionist. That said, I don't like for things to be released until I am completely satisfied with them. However, this is no excuse for not completing a task. But rest assured, there is no way that I will write to you about finishing and not practice what I preach. As a matter of fact, my unfinished items will be complete in a few days. I will follow through with them. But I can only imagine how much farther along I would have been in my ministry had I done those things when I should have.

HOW BAD DO YOU WANT IT?
Could it be that the greatness God has placed inside of you was supposed to be manifested a long time ago? Once you start, don't stop! Don't quit! Follow through and watch God work on your behalf. Keep this in mind as you start and work to finish. The greatness inside of you is not just for you. Others are depending on you to follow through. The world needs what God has placed inside of you. It's not just about you, but the world around you. If that doesn't motivate you to finish strong then I don't know what will. Imagine this: Once you finish strong, no one will ever be able to take that feeling of accomplishment away from you. No one will

ever take you seriously if you always start something but never finish.

For me, I had to reach a point where it would cause my family more detriment if I did not finish. For example, with this book, it was imperative that I finished because my word depended on it. I told certain people I was going to do it. Once I said it, they were expecting me to get it done. Had I just let it sit, you would not be reading it now. More so, I would have been looked upon as someone who couldn't keep his word. Without going back into my story too much, as a teenager, I lied a lot. Most of the lies I told were for survival since I had to pretend to be older than I was. But a majority of the others were lies just to lie! Being viewed as a liar as a teenager, I alienated myself from a lot of people. I refused to allow that to follow me into my adult life. I reached a point where lying wasn't necessary, nor did it make sense anymore. 1 Corinthians 13:11 says it best: *"When I was a child, I spake as a child, I understood as a child, I thought as a child: but when I became a man, I put away childish things."*

I had also reached a point in my life where I could no longer afford to be disobedient to the Lord. God had given me the vision to write this book. And since I viewed completing this book as if my family's life and me depended on it, I had to get to work. No excuses this time. I suggest you take the same attitude. Whether you are reading this book as a teenager or an adult, your word is your bond. If you say you're going to do something, get it done. Not only does your future success hinge upon it, but finishing something is a great character building moment as well. I challenge you to finish something. Not only will others believe in you, you'll also begin to believe in yourself.

CLOSE THE DEAL

If you were to ask any businessperson how important is it to close a deal, they would emphatically answer, "very important!" Without being able to close a deal, the only thing you are able to accomplish is a conversation. Can you imagine how many car dealerships would be out of business if they weren't able to sell any cars? Well, so it is with your success. In the world that we live in, it is necessary to know how to market or *"sell"* yourself in order to move forward. Sure, you could say that God is the one who would *"sell"* you to necessary individuals, as it is often said that, *"God doesn't call the qualified; He qualifies the called."* However, once God has qualified you through His preparation process, you're now ready to close the deal.

It is often said, *"don't sell yourself short."* As I have stated earlier, in your journey to achieve your call to something greater, set attainable, yet lofty goals for yourself. Then, through your consistency, make strides toward reaching your goals. The more you finish a project, the greater the next goal becomes. Before you know it, you'll be finishing like a champion! Go get it!

CHAPTER RECAP

If you're going to start this journey that you have been reading about in these last few chapters, then go all the way with it. Haven't you had enough failures in your life? Haven't you had more than your fair share of inconsistencies? Haven't you started too many projects, only to leave them unfinished? If so, finish strong!

Prove it to yourself that you not only have the courage to begin a task, but that you also have the stamina to finish a task all the way through.

To help you finish, one important factor I would suggest you use is your WHY. Think about why you are doing what you're doing. Whatever your reason is for wanting to walk in your call to something greater, use it to propel you to the next level. This will help you whenever you feel like you can't continue.

Also, don't be afraid to ask for help or advice along the way if you get stuck. Getting stuck is one thing; staying stuck is something totally different. Embrace where you are, but don't settle for where you are. If you're serious about making it to the next level, then you're going to have to learn how to finish.

After all, you can't make it to another level if you haven't finished the one you're currently on!

"Energy and persistence alter all things."
— *Albert Einstein*

GREATER>

CHAPTER 12
THE SOMETHING GREATER

And Jesus said unto him, No one, having put his hand to the plough, and looking back, is fit for the kingdom of God.
Luke 9:62 – (KJV)

So now that you've finished these 11 chapters, you should have some sense of the call that God has placed upon your life. You've done all the steps listed here. You've sought God, you've implemented the principles in chapters 3-11, now you're probably ready to hit the ground running. Hold on! As I've stated before, the way you start is equally as important as how you finish. In this final chapter, let me share with you the two main ways that people seek to achieve something greater. Once I do that, the choice will be yours.

GREATNESS WITH GOD
If you took my advice in chapters 3-6, you should understand that before you begin anything you should first seek the face of God. God is the One

who has had a plan for our entire lives before we even knew that we had a life to live. Given the fact that God has given us free will, our human nature often strays away from the plans that God has for us. But the moment we find ourselves back in the will of God is the moment our true calling in life gets back on track.

I would dare to say that, as long as God is on your side, nothing shall be impossible for you to achieve. Whether it be a better marriage, more finances, a better job, a healthier body, a closer walk with God, or anything else that your heart desires, if you partner with God, there are no limits. The key is making sure that you are consistent in your relationship with God. The Bible declares: *"For the LORD God is a sun and shield: the LORD will give grace and glory: no good thing will he withhold from them that walk uprightly."(Psalm 84:11)*

I don't know about you but I sure could use a whole lot of grace! But if you're anything like me, then you can't afford to miss out on the glory of God either. Think about this: God says that, *"no good thing will he withhold from them that walk uprightly."* Now, think about your dreams; think about your plans; think about your desires. Everything that you desire, should you be consistent in walking uprightly with

God, will come to pass. More than that, the things that you desire didn't even come from you originally, they came from God. That means that God wants you to be successful more than you want yourself to be successful since He gave you the dreams in the first place!

The very success you dream of—the yearning that you have inside of you to achieve something greater is obtainable through God. Now I realize that the text said we have to walk uprightly. I also realize that there is a text in the Bible that says: *"But we are all as an unclean thing, and all our righteousness's are as filthy rags…"* [Isaiah 64:6] But if you examine Psalm 84:11 more closely, the reason that we are able to walk uprightly is because God promised to give us His grace and His glory first. That's what one of Jesus' purposes was in coming to this earth; to give grace to those who did not deserve it. Remember Ephesians 2:8 from earlier in the book? We are saved by God's grace through our faith in God, because of this, we are able to walk uprightly. Since we are now walking uprightly, we are eligible to receive the call that God has placed upon us for something greater. Your call to something greater is directly tied to your relationship with God. If you sever your relationship with Him, you could possibly sever receiving your greatness from Him.

GREATNESS WITHOUT GOD

Some of you may be asking, "Do I have to be connected to God in order to achieve my dreams? Can't I do it by myself?" There are several people who believe that they have achieved greatness on their own. For whatever reason, these individuals do not have a relationship with God. But even without a relationship with the Lord, they consider themselves successful because of the success they have obtained in their careers. Others may look at what these individuals have accomplished and also view them as successful.

The Bible reminds us that there are two types of people; righteous and unrighteous. Now before we continue, I must caution you to be very careful here about judging someone else. No one has the right to judge anyone else's success in life. Moreover, no one has the right to judge another person's salvation. That responsibility is God's and God's alone. Keeping that in mind, we've already spoken about what's available to righteous people. However, what about unrighteous people? Are they eligible to go to a higher level? Can they too be called to something greater? The answer is, yes. These individuals can in fact be called to something greater. Whether they acknowledge God was the One who called them to another level or not is the question.

The Bible tells us that, "...*He maketh his sun to rise on the evil and on the good, and sendeth rain on the just and on the unjust.*" *[Matthew 5:45]* Unsaved people have contributed great things to society. However, just because a person may be unsaved does not automatically make them unintelligent. In case you haven't noticed, there are people in the world who have natural talent. They have the ability to do things that most people couldn't work hard enough to do. These types of people often rely on their "own" strengths and abilities to achieve things in life. On the surface, it looks like they have it all.

But if you take a closer look at these individuals, are they truly happy with their achievements? I know several people that fall into this category. They do not believe in God, yet, they have done very well for themselves in their careers. When something good happens to them, they attribute it to their work ethic. When something bad happens, they attribute it to bad luck. But what I've noticed more often than not is that they are continually chasing material things.

I heard a lady once say that she made a six-figure income but it still wasn't enough. There is a difference in being successful versus being content with your success. Those who are always aiming for the next level have great ambition. But that ambition can cause them to miss out on what's really important in life. If these people have families, the family usually suffers because of this person's ambition. They never find the time to spend with their spouses or children because they are working. If they are single, one could argue that the fact that they are single is because of their work.

If this is you, I would caution you that while it is necessary to provide for your family, your family is all you have. As such, you need to find a balance. This is true whether you believe in God or not. Whatever your belief system or motives, I simply advise not to allow those closest to you to suffer because you are constantly seeking more. Wanting more is not necessarily a bad thing depending on your motives for wanting more. But you also need to learn how to be content with what you have. Contentment is a necessary element of success.

THE CHOICE IS YOURS
God is not going to force Himself on anyone. He has given us free will; because of that free will, we can choose success with God or without God. But what I have found to be true for me is that every time I try to do something on my own, I always mess it up. However, when I choose to work in cooperation

with God on a particular thing, it always works out better for me in the end. My advice to you would be to make a choice. Do you want to achieve success on your own, or do you want to achieve success with the God who made you to be successful? By default, not choosing is choosing.

FINAL RECAP

Everyone has been called to something greater. No matter who you are, you have definitely been called. It is my prayer that as you have read this book, you have now received the motivation to answer your call to something greater. After all, what good is it to receive a call but never answer? The purpose of receiving a call is to answer the call. If I can use a telephone analogy, some of us are defeating the purpose of our phones. When someone calls us we have the option to either answer the call or let it go to voicemail. But if you let most of your calls go to voicemail, why is it necessary to have a phone? For those of you with cell phones, if you hit the ignore button on the phone whenever you receive a call, why pay the monthly bill for a phone?

The same is true with us as humans. Every one of us has been given a call. Too many of us have let the call go to "voicemail" or we hit the "ignore" button. In either case, not answering the call could be detrimental. Not only to us personally but to our loved ones as well.

Say what you will, but my honest opinion is that God is on the other end of the phone calling us, waiting for each of us to pick up. Don't believe in God?

Okay. But that "thing" that is inside of you driving you to go to another level, where do you think that comes from? I suggest to you that, *"if it seem evil unto you to serve the LORD, choose you this day whom ye will serve..."* [Joshua 24:15] I can only tell you for me, it's definitely God. And because of everything that I have been through in my life, I have come to the conclusion that, *"as for me and my house, we will serve the LORD."* [Joshua 24:15]

Jeremiah understood that God was the answer. He understood that without God he was nothing. Before Jeremiah began his ministry, he realized that if God was not with him (as evidenced by God touching Jeremiah's mouth with a hot coal placing His words inside of him), there really wouldn't be anything to say.

You have been given a great opportunity to go to another level. Not satisfied with where you are? Answer your call to something greater! Upset for not following through on certain things? Answer your call to something greater! Missed out on too many opportunities in life? Answer your call to something greater! Feeling like there is more for you to do in this world? Then answer your call to something greater! Discover your greatness. Seek God's will for your life. Have the faith to pursue your greatness.

Believe in God's will for your life. Have mental toughness along the way. Get your mind right!. Make the transition to your greatness. Don't speak about it, be about it. Learn how to deal with the criticism of others; some will be bad, some will be good. Develop a support system; be there for others so others can be there for you. Look the part; act according to what your future holds. Don't procrastinate; don't let your potential greatness pass you by. Finish strong; go hard or go home! Finally, recognize THE something greater in your life just like you did at the beginning. Your greatness starts with God and ends with God.

I pray this book has blessed you. It is my prayer that you desire nothing more in your life than to walk in the favor and anointing of God. After all, you are - **"Called to Something Greater!"**

Be challenged. Be motivated. Be encouraged. Be GREAT!

> *"There is no greater agony than bearing*
> *an untold story inside of you."*
> *Maya Angelou*

THE SOMETHING GREATER

GREATER>

BOOK DARRELL TODAY!

Looking for Speaking, Preaching, or Workshops, contact Darrell at 404.259.1774.

- Facebook @darrellpalmes
- Twitter @darrellpalmes
- YouTube @dpalmes

www.darrellpalmes.org

www.caringtouchministries.org

NOTES

NOTES

NOTES

NOTES

NOTES

SPIRIT REIGN
PUBLISHING
A Division of Spirit Reign Communications